What people are saying about …

The Juggling Act

"Pat Gelsinger holds one of the most challenging and influential positions in the digital world, and he is a committed Christian giving significant time to family and ministry. If there is anyone qualified to show people how to balance a busy, multifaceted life, it is Pat."

Steve Douglass, president and chairman of
the board of Campus Crusade for Christ

"Pat Gelsinger's book should be on everyone's must-read list. Not only is it inspirational in chronicling one man's rise to the top of his field, but it also lays out a blueprint to follow in balancing God, family, and work in everyday life. People who are struggling to jump-start their careers will find the chapter on creating a personal mission statement essential. Those who struggle to find ten minutes out of each workday just to breathe need to read this book to hone their organizational skills, prioritize jobs, develop a system to monitor their progress and develop laserlike focus."

Ronny Svenhard, CEO and chairman of
the board of Svenhard's Swedish Bakery

"I have known Pat and Linda Gelsinger for more than twenty-five years, performed their wedding, know their children, and watched with abundant joy the global impact of their family. This deeply personal book is authentic, powerful, refreshingly radical, and will forever change your life if you apply its principles. *The Juggling Act* demonstrates in a practical way that your life can have fulfilling balance even in the midst of demanding schedules and responsibilities. I wholeheartedly endorse it, especially for those seeking to balance faith, family, and work."

Dr. Bryce Jessup, president of William Jessup University

"Gelsinger's *The Juggling Act* avoids simple platitudes. Instead, the author offers personal insights and practical tips for professionals seeking a deeper relationship with God, a flourishing family life, and a career worthy of a calling."

David W. Miller, PhD, executive director of Yale Center for Faith & Culture, and author of *God at Work*

"Here's a terrific guide to managing your time and setting your priorities in a wise and biblical manner. Pat Gelsinger has learned from experience how important it is to put faith and family first, and he graciously shares his journey with us. You don't need to be an executive to benefit from this book. There's something here for everyone."

Jim Daly, president and CEO of Focus on the Family, and author of *Finding Home*

"Once again Pat has challenged me to do more than I ever thought possible, encouraged me to reach for meaningful goals, and reminded me to be so thankful for what I have been given. I am not sure which story moved my emotions more, the awkward dinner with Linda or your walking into the Intel microprocessor design team and sharing your ideas. Thanks for taking the risk to be a 'clear witness' to so many, especially to me."

Kevin Compton, general partner of Kleiner Perkins Caufield & Byers

"Reading through this book, I can tell that Pat is very close to God. He has the wisdom and discipline to obey God's commands, which has enabled him to become an excellent and godly husband, father, and employee. I do greatly respect Pat's persistence and discipline. I am sure that those who read this book will benefit greatly from this real-life experience of a successful executive."

Charlene Chien, president of First International Computer, Inc.

"Pat Gelsinger knows how hard it is to juggle work, family, and faith. Sharing from his own life and heart, Pat has written an honest, solid guide that will challenge and inspire all of us to live more balanced, meaningful lives."

Bas Vanderzalm, president of Medical Teams International

THE
JUGGLINGACT

THE
JUGGLINGACT

BRINGING BALANCE TO YOUR
FAITH, FAMILY, AND WORK

·······

PAT GELSINGER

David C Cook®
transforming lives together

THE JUGGLING ACT
Published by David C Cook
4050 Lee Vance View
Colorado Springs, CO 80918 U.S.A.

David C Cook Distribution Canada
55 Woodslee Avenue, Paris, Ontario, Canada N3L 3E5

David C Cook U.K., Kingsway Communications
Eastbourne, East Sussex BN23 6NT, England

The graphic circle C logo is a registered trademark of David C Cook.

The Web site addresses recommended throughout this book are offered as a
resource to you. These Web sites are not intended in any way to be or imply an
endorsement on the part of David C Cook, nor do we vouch for their content.

LCCN 2008933680
ISBN 978-1-4347-6874-2
eISBN 978-1-4347-6515-4

First edition published by Life Journey under the title *Balancing Your Family,
Faith & Work* © 2003 Pat Gelsinger, ISBN 978-0-7814-3899-5

The Team: Susan Tjaden, Amy Kiechlin, Jack Campbell, and Karen Athen
Cover Design: Nate Salciccioli, The DesignWorks Group
Cover Photo: Steve Gardner, PixelWorks Studios

Printed in the United States of America
Second Edition 2008

2 3 4 5 6 7 8 9 10

090115-CS

THIS BOOK IS A PRODUCT OF MY LIFE AND
THAT OF MY WIFE AND FAMILY.

· · · · ·

To our kids, Elizabeth, Josiah, Nathan, and Micah: Thank
you for being great kids, challenging me when I failed,
and encouraging me to be the best dad you deserve.

· · · · ·

To my mentors like Andy Grove, Steve Menefee, and
Bryce Jessup: Your commitment to helping and making me
be better along the way has made me what I am.

· · · · ·

To the many friends along the journey of life: Your touch to
my life and family will be measured only in eternity.

· · · · ·

Most of all, to my darling wife, Linda: In this second version, you
stepped WAY out of your comfort zone and contributed part of your
life story with mine. You've been my perfect mate, my balance,
my friend, and my love. My Lady, you are the delight of my life.

Contents

· · · · ·

Acknowledgments

. . . . .

This topic and book have as much to do with who I am and my life as they do with who my family members are and their lives. Thus I must acknowledge each one's life as it reflects into my own. While in many cases I am the visible face at work, at church, and in the leadership of our home, often the real substance and strength lie in the family that backs me up day and night. You might look at aspects of my life and be impressed, but the real heroes are a supportive wife and children who have been blessed by God and are a great blessing to me.

Of course the greatest acknowledgment goes to my dear wife, Linda. On one anniversary, a wave of emotion came over me, causing me to pronounce regarding our relationship: "While it seems we were married just yesterday, it's like we've been together forever." In many ways that defines our relationship: still fresh, new, and powerful, yet it's hard to remember life before she came into my world. I've grown in compassion and affection for her as the years have proceeded.

Linda is the backbone of the Gelsinger household. As my travels take me to and fro on far too many occasions, she more than holds the fort down. With a clear and certain view of what is right and what is wrong, she is ready both to encourage and challenge me when I get out of balance in any aspect of my life. While this may sound trite, it is more than true that this message and this book would never have been possible without her. Our kids are turning out well because of her commitment and leadership of our household. One friend of ours said to Linda, "I should just have you raise my kids too." It was said in jest, but it was a great compliment as she recognized through our kids the imprint of a dedicated mother. To Linda, my Lady and Love, thank you.

The support, love, and affection of our children bring me both joy and delight. Elizabeth, thank you for being a young Christian woman who demonstrates God's character in your daily life. While I've appreciated the times I've been able to teach you, you've taught me much and brought me even greater joy in return. How I enjoy watching God transform you from girl to teen to woman. You are a great elementary schoolteacher with a heart for kids and a talent to teach them. God will use you and your skills in powerful ways both overseas and close to home as you remain committed to let him be the God of your life. Oh yes, and Mom gives you an extra thanks for all of your special help to her on the editing of the afterword!

Josiah, I enjoy your quick thinking and intelligence. Watching you grow to adulthood is both exciting and frightening. Every game I watch you play makes me proud to be your father. You have become a man too quickly. Thank you for challenging me both to be home and to be *really* home when I am there. As you begin your career as a youth minister, I'm anxious to see how God will use you and the lives you will touch.

Nathan, how refreshing is your seemingly perpetual joy and enthusiasm for life. I cannot describe the pleasure of seeing so many characteristics of my own being lived again in you. I look forward to watching how God will work in your life as you follow his gifting of you for music and his call on your life to enter full-time ministry.

Thank you for making our home forever exciting, interesting, and always unique.

Micah, thank you for your determination and dogged pursuit of what is right and true. You are racing far too quickly to manhood and independence. Mom and I aren't ready yet for an empty nest; but, alas, time refuses to let you wait. Thank you for your love and your joy of being with me and doing just about anything I'm doing. I pray that God will lead you mightily—maybe to the mission field, maybe to somewhere else—as you seek to honor his will and direction for your life.

Finally, I thank Bryce Jessup, our pastor for many years, the man who married Linda and me, and who has been a mentor, a mentee, and best of all a friend. Also, you are the one I've been able to encourage to "not be a wimp" when considering how big our God really is. More than any other, you've encouraged—nay, *demanded*—I write this text. Thank you for editing, commenting, and constantly e-mailing me the message, "That's good! Add it to your book." I look forward to continued years of encouragement and mentoring. Thank you for the years of your great wisdom poured into my life. Most of all, thank you for being a friend and brother in Christ.

Foreword

by *Ken Blanchard*

. . . . .

I should have known I would love *The Juggling Act* because it was sent to me by my Bible coach, Richard Case, who meets on the phone with me and four of my colleagues and friends every Wednesday morning at 6:00 a.m., California time. Rich knows me as well as anyone and has helped me with my own "juggling act," so he knew I would relate to and learn from Pat's story.

After reading *The Juggling Act*, I am excited about meeting Pat someday. Why? Because we have a lot of things in common. First of all, we both married above ourselves. Without Pat's wife, Linda, and my wife, Margie, we would never be where we are today. God knew we needed great mates to keep us balanced and our priorities in order. Don't miss Linda's afterword, "Insights from a Juggler's Wife."

Second, we are both confused about the difference between work and play, which makes balancing life more difficult. The comfort in it is that we're probably doing what God wants us to do, because I don't think the good Lord put us here to be clock watchers. If you find yourself saying, "Thank God it's Friday," or feeling depressed on Sunday nights, you might be better off finding something else to do. The important choice when you love what you do for work is whether you're going to be a peak performer or a workaholic. Charles Garfield made this distinction for me years ago: Workaholics never know how to shut the motor down. They sneak their cell phones onto the golf course. When they are home, they are never really home. On the other hand, peak performers might work twenty-eight hours a day for a period of time, but then they shut the motor down and do something else. They will stay in the car in their home driveway to finish their last phone call so when they walk in their house they can be there for whomever is home—spouse, kids, relatives, or friends. Pat Gelsinger was a workaholic who has learned to be a peak performer just as I have, and marrying above ourselves really helped that to happen. Pat's struggles and victory with balance will help you if you tend to get your life out of balance like we do.

Third, Pat and I have both learned that our work is also a ministry. I'll never forget the response Norman Vincent Peale, with whom I had the pleasure of writing *The Power of Ethical Management*, gave me when I asked him, "Should I quit what I'm doing as a business consultant and writer and go back to divinity school and become a preacher?" Norman's response to my question was quick and to the point: "Absolutely not; you have a huge congregation in the business world and we don't have enough preachers there." Pat Gelsinger certainly has learned that, and has found that he can do more good for the Lord where he is planted, as a top manager at Intel, than he ever could as an official preacher.

Fourth, Pat and I have both learned that your actions are more powerful than your words, even though we do not hide that we are followers of Jesus. I think we both would argue that the next great evangelistic movement in the world will be demonstration, not proclamation. If we want to have more people follow Jesus, then as Christians we ought to behave differently. As you read *The Juggling Act*, you'll see how Pat Gelsinger lives and walks his faith in the marketplace.

And finally, keeping our priorities in order is a constant challenge for Pat and me. I was on a speaking platform one time with Tom Landry, the great Dallas Cowboys football coach when someone asked him, "Coach, how have you been able to stay so calm in the midst of a crazy, competitive game like football?" Landry said, "It's easy, I have my priorities in order. First comes God, then my wife, then my kids, and then, finally, my work. So if I lose a game on Sunday, I have a lot left over." He went on to say, "Unfortunately, there are a lot of coaches who, when they lose on Sunday, are devastated, because who they are *is* their job." I have learned that what most men think after they say, "I do," is, "Now that the marriage job is done, I can get back to work." Listening to Pat wrestle with this tendency will help you—it certainly has helped me. And watching how Linda has avoided the problem many women get into after they say "I do" is helpful too. Most women want to take on their husband as their missionary work and change him. Just as Pat has learned to back off work sometimes to court Linda and focus on the kids, Linda has learned to let the Lord change Pat while her job is to love and support him. Great learnings here for everyone.

I could go on and on. I really got into *The Juggling Act,* and I think you will too if you're wrestling with your own juggling act, as well as trying to have both a successful and significant life.

Thank you, Pat, and you, too, Linda, for sharing your story. Margie and I look forward to giving you both a big hug someday. God bless.

— KEN BLANCHARD,

coauthor of *The One Minute Manager* and *Lead Like Jesus*

Disclaimer: The contents of this book are solely the personal views of Pat Gelsinger and are not views representing Intel Corporation.

Introduction

.....

I'm Pat—a farm boy turned senior executive of a Fortune 100 company where I am responsible for thousands of employees and a large portion of Intel's business. I am also the father of four nearly grown kids and the husband for the past twenty-five years to my wonderful wife, Linda. I am active in the Christian community, both in our church and in various parachurch organizations. I speak often in public forums, making clear my Christian faith to the business and high-tech community on a regular basis.

I've made numerous mistakes and have had my share of failures along the way. Often these are of my own doing, and sometimes they are God's way of teaching and maturing me to the next level. After juggling between the numerous and often-overwhelming demands of these many roles, I've gained some experience and wisdom that I hope will provide some utility in your life.

This is a new edition of what was originally published as *Balancing Family, Faith & Work*. While you will find many similarities to the first edition, each chapter has been updated, and much has been added. Most important, Linda has offered some of her personal perspectives in the afterword. This provides both a spouse's and a woman's perspective to the topics discussed herein. A chapter has also been added on "Integrating Faith, Family, and Work."

The first edition of this book grew out of a message that I gave in speech form to many men's groups, business groups, and gatherings of professionals across the United States. I've also had the opportunity to present these ideas in India, Taiwan, Malaysia, China, Germany, Singapore, Hong Kong, and Japan. The response has been overwhelmingly positive. Somehow this message has found a universal resonance in the lives of those in the audience.

Our world today is increasingly busy. It appears that men and women in the rat race, the dot-com craze, the home-versus-business trap, and those just struggling to keep up are crying out for some way to manage the increasing busyness and craziness of our times. I've heard it said that Satan doesn't need to deceive us; he just needs to keep us busy. All that busyness, of course, can lead to an ineffective witness, career struggles, family strife, divorce, and ultimate failure in one's personal and professional life. We've all heard stories of a respected businessperson's marriage ending in divorce, or maybe a bitter family feud about the dividing of an estate or a family business. As you read those stories, you pause to wonder if it was worth it. While on one hand you might yearn for that business success, you also have to ponder the costs and consequences. If you were that successful, would you have a different outcome than the personal or family train wreck you see in those "successful" people? While you might crave the glamour of the lives of some who are on the front pages of tabloids and business journals, would you really want the family chaos that most have received in the course of the achievement?

During our family's summer vacation in 1999, I read the book *Half Time* by Bob Buford, which has a simple and powerful message: going from success to significance.[1] If you haven't read that work yet, I highly recommend it. Read it through when you have a bit of time to ponder your life and career. As we've labored through a significant portion of our time on earth, what are we seeking? The next rung of the ladder toward career success? The next material acquisition that declares success to our friends and neighborhood? The acceptance letter for our children at the top-name school? Some other form of worldly recognition?

Buford's book is good, and yet terrible, to read on a vacation. Instead of the mindless relaxation I was planning during my break, it challenged me to a period of deep self-reflection and consideration of my life's purpose. As I analyzed myself, I, too, confronted the question of whether I was investing my life in the right things. Was I out for success or significance? Should I consider a dramatic restructuring of my life as Buford had done? Should I step out of the corporate world entirely and simply "be home" to focus single-mindedly on my family?

Early in my life, I had seen powerfully that my career and position at Intel were exactly where God wanted me to be. Thus, while the idea of getting out of the rat race and the juggling life was attractive, I knew that wasn't God's purpose for me at the time. Instead, I was sensing this increasingly enthusiastic response to the message of my life. God wanted to use me in my position at Intel, together with what I had learned as a juggler of time and priorities, to influence others for his kingdom.

I've heard some people reflecting on Buford's book say, "First you focus on being successful. Then, after you've achieved success, you focus on being significant." While I disagree with that summary of Buford's book, I can see how some might have drawn that simple conclusion. The book you are now reading isn't about stepping out of the work world. No, it's about being a successful Christian and having a fulfilled life and healthy family while being in the working world. As you will see, you are called to be a minister while in the workforce and living in the marketplace. God doesn't intend for us to delay a desire for significance or for "doing ministry" until after we retire; he calls us to be heads of our families and to be ministry leaders while we are still in the workplace.

After speaking at a Timeout conference in the fall of 2000 on this subject, I was challenged by a number of the participants to write a book. One in particular said to me, "I have heard no one with as much to say as you do who hasn't written it down."

As my busy, juggling lifestyle had plenty of demands already, I was reluctant to undertake this project. Having coauthored a book once before, *Programming the 80386* (great for the nightstand—it will surely send you off to a good night's sleep),[2] I was well acquainted with the amount of work involved in writing a quality book.

However, after numerous individuals encouraged me in this regard, I decided to give it a shot. In the spare minutes, late hours, and long plane flights, I began to write. In fact, I undertook the writing process without conferring with Linda. I knew she'd be uncomfortable with another project being added to my plate. I'm always one to try to do more and squeeze in just one more thing. *(Hmm, thirty minutes until it's time to leave, I can certainly get one more project done!)* Thus, knowing her almost certain reaction, I determined to finish a draft in my spare time to assure her it wouldn't be yet another burden on the family. When I finally did raise the idea of writing a book, her reaction was about what I expected. You can imagine her surprise when I informed her that, indeed, I had already finished a first draft. Instead of being proud of my squeezing this additional project into my spare time, she felt instead I was sneaky or devious doing this behind her back!

During my once-every-seven-year sabbatical from Intel, I found enough spare time to get a near-final work completed on the first edition. Just one last trip to Asia and it was ready to give to the publisher.

Now as I'm writing this second edition, I'm not as foolish or sneaky as I was with the first edition. Linda is sitting right next to me as I type. She is working on her afterword, and we've integrated our skills and experiences into a shared work. I consider this to be progress in our relationship, as well as growth in how God is using us both in ministry.

The first edition challenged and encouraged numerous people. Many have commented that they are using particular suggestions, writing their mission statements, or engaging with mentors in their lives. How encouraging it is to hear such stories of life-impacting and sometimes life-changing results!

My prayer is that you might find this book useful in your personal juggling act. If just a few more of you find this second edition useful in your lives, the many hours of typing will be more than justified.

BOOK STRUCTURE

The book is broken into nine chapters. The first is, simply, my testimony. As I've delivered this message as a lecture, I've found that when people hear my story, the points of the remaining chapters take on greater meaning and clarity. Often people will make comments like "If you can do that, certainly I can manage my own situation." You'll soon see that I've been extraordinarily blessed through a series of what some would call coincidences. But I see them as blessings from the divine Creator and Overseer of the universe. As my father would say about himself, "I'm not sure why I've been chosen to be so blessed, but I have been." While I fear a testimony of such overwhelming blessing might come through as pride or arrogance, it is what God has done in my life. Hopefully, through reading it, you might learn just a bit about who I am, who my wife and family are, what I've accomplished at Intel and in our church, and what God has done in each of these areas of my life.

Chapters 2 through 8 provide seven specific principles for becoming a master juggler of life's priorities. Each principle is illustrated by examples from my life, and each chapter ends with several questions to help you apply this material to your own life or possibly in a group setting.

As a special conclusion to the book, Linda offers her perspective on living with a master juggler. Whenever I've spoken, individuals have always felt like they've become acquainted with my wife, whether or not she was present. Many have asked about her perspective or have even gone so far as to say, "Now we want to hear from Linda!" Well, in answer to that request, this section gives some of her unique perspective on the subjects of being a supportive spouse, what it means to balance, what some of the challenges that juggling has afforded, and how she has coped with them.

QUESTIONS

I've included a set of questions at the end of each chapter. These are meant for personal use as you ponder your own situation and apply the chapter material to your life and current situation. These could also be used in a class setting or small group as discussion topics; some have used them as formal study material when using the book as a study guide. Most of the questions are taken from those I've received as I've presented this material over the years. While they are included here simply in question form, in the appendix I've also included each question with the answer that I would give from my personal life.

Many of these questions are personal and have no right or wrong answer. They're meant as much to provoke thought, discussion, and action as to have you provide a specific correct answer. I'd encourage you to answer them and share your thoughts with your spouse, close friend, and/or mentors, and then begin to work on your priorities for your own life.

• • • • •

As a born-again believer in the Lord Jesus Christ, my faith is at the foundation of who I am, what I stand for, what I dream of accomplishing, and what I desire to become as a man. My faith is an inextricable element of my personality and my life's experiences. I write from a Christian perspective and make no apologies for my faith. As I first started writing the book, I thought it might have broader audience appeal if I wrote from a more neutral perspective. I couldn't do it. I simply couldn't write a book that gave an in-depth view of my family and who I really am without reflecting my faith in a central and substantive manner.

With that in mind, however, I recognize that some, hopefully many, who read this book may not share my faith. I hope and believe this book can still be of use to you. In particular, chapters 4 through 6 can be applied wholly and with little hesitation regardless of what faith, if any, you might choose to follow. However, you might find chapters 1–3, 7, and 8 a bit arduous. While I don't apologize for who I am in these areas of the book, I do hope you'll still find them useful as you journey through life and attempt to be a master juggler, one who can balance and integrate all aspects of life. Of course, my greatest joy would be that you also might choose to trust and serve the risen Savior, Jesus Christ.

Finally, please take a look at the accompanying Web site: www.patgelsinger.com. From time to time, I will be updating it with complementary study materials as well as my speaking schedule. I hope you are able to join me at one of these events! You can also see some video comments I've given on www.iquestions.com as well as a TV series that includes me as one of its features a number of business executives (www.secretsofsuccess.com).

1

. . . . .

From Farm Country
to Silicon Valley

. . . . .

ROBESONIA IS AN IDYLLIC little borough in the heart of Pennsylvania Dutch country. It's where I was born and raised—and where I learned the meaning of hard work. Both of my parents' families were dairy, cattle, and crop farmers. My mother was from a family of eleven, and several of her siblings never made it past infancy. My dad was from a family of nine children. He was a twin at number seven/eight in the family. Both Mom and Dad were of similar Pennsylvania Dutch upbringing. Both were raised on farms. Both learned English as their second language. While they grew up some sixty miles apart, each walked to the nearest one-room schoolhouse for their first-through-eighth-grade education. For both of my parents, their large families made up a high percentage of the student body in the tiny one-room schoolhouse that provided the entirety of their formal education. Neither was given the opportunity to pursue an education beyond eighth grade.

As my dad's siblings reached the age of maturity and marriage, they moved into farming with a bit of financial assistance from Grandpa. Grandpa helped son #1, son #2, daughter #1, and so on, but when finally getting to my dad, he said, "You're on your own, Son, we already have enough farms in the family." Thus, my father began his farming career by working for his brothers.

There's always more than enough work to do on a farm. Thus, Dad was more than welcome to help out a couple of my uncles. This worked wonderfully for quite a few years. Then, as his older brothers began having their own families, and their children reached the age of maturity and took on the responsibilities of the family farms, Dad became less central to the operations of my uncles' farms. On several occasions Dad looked into buying a farm, but he was never quite the high bidder, or the loan didn't quite materialize, or he just didn't have enough financial support from Grandpa to go forward with the purchase. Thus, he never did acquire a farm of his own.

I enjoyed the hard work of my uncles' farms. Further, I always liked working with my dad. Had Dad ever acquired a farm of his own, I'd be there to this day, working with him on the family homestead. Instead of being an expert in computer chips, I'd be quite knowledgeable in cow chips!

I learned much from my dad and my farming uncles, aunts, and cousins. It's hard to be closely associated with a farming environment and not develop a deep and powerful work ethic. Up early every day, hard manual labor from dawn to dusk, and late to bed, totally exhausted from a hard day's toil.

While Dad continued to work on the farm with my uncles, he

took on a full-time position at the local steel mill. Since that wasn't enough to make ends meet and keep him busy, he was also a township supervisor overseeing most of their road building and maintenance. For almost all of my formative years, I saw him working these three jobs simultaneously. He worked hard to provide a lifestyle and environment for his family that was better than the one he was raised in. To this day, I consider myself somewhat lazy compared to him. In many ways, he's one of the heroes of my life.

We attended church every Sunday. My family and many of my immediate relatives attended the United Church of Christ in nearby Wernersville. I was baptized at six days old and only missed a Sunday under rare circumstances of illness. We polished our shoes Saturday nights, got up Sunday mornings, put on our jackets and ties, and went to church. Dad disliked being late for church, so we rarely ever were. This was just the way it was, and I was not about to disrupt the family's routine.

I was formally confirmed when I was twelve years old. This was the process by which one became a full member of the congregation. Since we were baptized as infants, this was the point where you would make a public declaration of membership into the congregation. I became president of the youth group at fourteen. By all outward appearances, I was a shining example of a Christian young man. I was at church every Sunday, knew the hymns well, did my turn as altar boy, was confirmed, and was president of the youth group. What else could you want or expect from a young guy? Some years later when my then-wife-to-be, Linda, asked if I was a Christian, the reply without hesitation or doubt was, "Yes!" And I proceeded to recite this same list of evidences why that assertion was true. Like many today, I was certain my works and achievements qualified me for a position in God's eyes. How naive and wrong I was.

But the reality of my life was far different. While I was by all outward signs a perfect specimen of a Christian young man on Sundays, the remainder of the week was a different story. By the time I was seventeen, I had experimented with many of the temptations of our age. Several of the guys I hung around with were not the kind of company you would want for friends of your children.

Living a lie was fun, daring, and challenging. I liked being seen as the perfect boy on Sundays. Every mother and grandmother would compliment me, and many would convey their desire for me to be their own each Sunday. Of course, keeping the mothers and grandmothers on my side was most beneficial for positioning myself with some of the young ladies that I had my eye on at the time.

Looking back, I would compare my life then to those coin bins that sit at the doorways of some diners and restaurants. You drop a coin in the top and it goes spiraling slowly downward. While the coin might "think" the ride is wonderful, thrilling, and fun, the end point is absolute and final; gravity makes sure it lands in the hole at the bottom 100 percent of the time. For those in such a lifestyle as I was, the end is equally final—a hole at the end of life called hell. That's the path I was on, and I was by all appearances enjoying the ride and making very good time.

God had, however, blessed me with a good mind, and he began to use it to steer me in a different direction. Because Dad didn't have his own farm for me to inherit, I would have to pursue a different career path. I considered a variety of options and decided to give electronics a try. Partially out of typical high school boredom, and partially out of good math skills and a general interest in electronics, I began attending Berks Vocational Technical School in the afternoons of my sophomore and junior years of high school. The teacher of the class, Howard Buck, was particularly encouraging to me. He challenged my lifestyle on more than one occasion, and as he saw some of the individuals I was hanging out with and my decaying lifestyle, he became concerned. He saw considerable talent in me and was very concerned about the apparent squandering of those talents. One day he even pulled me aside to encourage me on a more fruitful path. While he is now deceased, I am grateful for his willingness to take such a proactive role.

It was during this time that I accidentally took the Lincoln Technical Institute's electronics technology scholarship exam. The exam was intended for seniors but somehow I ended up taking it during my junior year in high school. Surprisingly, I won the scholarship and was entitled to two years of free tuition. Because our family was considered lower-middle class economically, a full-tuition scholarship was very enticing indeed. Today, I clearly see this episode as a bit of divine intervention in my life.

Winning the scholarship did pose a certain difficulty though: I wasn't yet a senior and wouldn't be graduating from high school for another year and a half. However, the scholarship was offered for only the following school year. Thus, a chapter of my life began to unfold that I would have never anticipated.

THE JUGGLING BEGINS

With a scholarship and greater challenges, opportunities, and freedom in front of me, I skipped my last year of high school and began working toward my associate's degree at Lincoln Technical Institute at the age of seventeen. I commuted for a few months, but after I was in a car accident, my parents and I decided that I should move into an apartment immediately adjacent to the school. While my roommates were generally nice guys, they were even more wordly than I, active in drinking, drugs, and rock 'n' roll.

While in hindsight I don't recommend people rush into life quite as quickly as I did, God was clearly working my poor choices toward a higher calling for my life. He was about to begin a mighty and amazing work in me.

Not only did I start working on my two-year degree at seventeen, but I also accelerated my coursework at Lincoln Tech. Instead of taking six quarters, I doubled up classes one quarter and finished in five. Also, while it was fine with my high school for me to skip a year, I needed to have a few more credits to complete my high school requirements. Thus, I also attended some night classes in calculus, English, and history at the local community college, Lehigh Valley Community College. This was the beginning of the overflowing schedule that would become common for me, as you will see. I was intense and disciplined. Given my farming background, I was comfortable working hard and sleeping only five hours a night during the week. (Admittedly, I continue this kind of intense schedule to this day.)

During this period, I also began part-time work. While my classes were paid for by my scholarship, I needed money for rent, gas, and books. The local radio and TV station, WFMZ, hired me primarily to do equipment maintenance and repair, but I also managed to get a few weekend night shifts of keeping music on the air, doing a weather announcement or two, and keeping the TV programs and commercials on the air. After doubling up on classes, taking evening classes, and now working evenings and weekends, my skills for a career as a master juggler were already taking shape.

At Lincoln Tech I had my first experience with computers. As soon as I started using one, I was hooked. I now knew what I wanted to do with my career. I began playing with a Radio Shack TRS 80, my first RSA 1802, and other simple training computers available at Lincoln Tech. While I was enthusiastic about electronics in general, computers became my passion. I consumed everything I could find on the subject.

In my last quarter at Lincoln I began to interview for electronics technician positions. I interviewed with a variety of East Coast companies like IBM and Western Electric. While I really wasn't interested in leaving the East Coast, I also decided to talk with a West Coast company named Intel, which had come to recruit technicians. Generally, Intel didn't recruit on the East Coast, but they were growing rapidly and there was an industry-wide shortage of technicians. I was the last interviewee in what had been a long day for Ron J. Smith, an engineering manager for Intel at the time. He had interviewed twelve candidates that day. For any of you who have ever done any interviewing, you know that after about five or six candidates, you barely can recall one from another. After about nine or ten, it's hard to tell male from female ... and I was number twelve on his agenda! His reactions were reflected in the brief summary he wrote about me: "Smart, very aggressive, and somewhat arrogant— he'll fit right in."

From this interview, I received an invitation to visit Intel. I was eighteen years old and had never been on an airplane. Outside of a few trips to neighboring states and one trip to the Niagara Falls in Canada, our family had not traveled very far from home at all and certainly not all the way across the country! After careful and thoughtful consideration that lasted about two nanoseconds, I accepted the invitation for my first-ever plane flight to the growing and already-famous Silicon Valley of California.

While I was off on my interview trip to California, my mother was having major surgery. On the day of my return, I walked into her hospital room, and the instant she saw me, she knew I was bound for the West. In one of several marvelous, divine coincidences in my life, this was the only year that Intel ever came recruiting at Lincoln Tech. Had I not "accidentally" taken that scholarship exam, I'd never have had the opportunity to interview with Intel.

I thus graduated with my high school class in June of that year, finished my associate's degree from Lincoln Tech at the top of my class in August, and left for California in October to start working at Intel. To say the least, 1979 had been a most amazing year for me.

OFF TO CALIFORNIA

Despite the objections of my relatives, I packed up my sparse belongings and started the trek to California. I knew no one there except for a couple of guys from Lincoln Tech who took jobs at Intel at the same time I did. Thus, the suggestion to get a house together was easy to accept. While my salary seemed like a fortune for an East Coast farm boy, I quickly found that living in California was much more expensive than I expected. I could not even come close to affording an apartment of my own. Furthermore, having someone familiar around was comforting for this eighteen-year-old who was much too far from home.

Jack was a guitar-playing, pot-smoking, drug-using, hot-rodding, rock 'n' roller. Bob was a neo-Nazi kind of guy who collected guns, grenades, and bomb materials. As you might expect, spirituality wasn't a strong point of our bachelor-trio home. Jack and Bob; Bongs and Bombs—what a great set of peers and housemates!

Because my roommate Jack immediately convinced me to repaint my eyesore-of-a-car, I was without transportation for my first few weeks in California. Intel was just a few blocks away so it was easy to walk to work. However, not having a car meant I would need to walk to the nearest church rather than seeking out a UCC church or a Lutheran church that would have been true to my roots. In keeping with the habit of my youth to be in church on Sunday, I took a stroll to Santa Clara Christian Church, which was just a few blocks down the street.

At the end of the first service I attended there, two young women, Karen and Linda, came up to greet this young visitor. They seemed a bit giggly but were friendly. When I identified myself as having just moved to California and started with Intel, Linda immediately asked, "Do you eat in the cafeteria?" This question struck me as odd for a first question to ask someone you are welcoming to church. Thus, in my response, I gave her a very perplexed look. This expression sent the two of them off giggling.

A couple of silly girls had absolutely zero appeal to me. It turns out that Linda worked for the food-services company that ran the cafeterias at Intel, so her seemingly odd question wasn't really silly as I assumed, but it certainly did start us off on the wrong foot.

Linda didn't find me any more appealing than I initially found her. She looked at me as a smart-aleck, immature kid. In contrast, she was three years older, had been living on her own for two years, and was certainly far more mature. We couldn't have been further from love at first sight.

It was another one of those divine coincidences. Had it been a couple of weeks later, when my car would be back in driving condition, I probably never would have chosen to attend this church. Instead, I would have certainly gone looking for something closer to my denominational heritage. However, the youth group quickly welcomed me in to join them in their various activities. This young lady named Linda was almost always there. Thus, we began to strike up an acquaintance despite our initial, mutual distaste for each other.

Despite the fact that my roommates and I were quite the bachelors and not particularly domesticated, we decided to have a Thanksgiving feast for our few friends in the area. I invited Linda over to join us. After the meal and cleanup, we went for a nice walk around the neighborhood and discussed a wide range of personal and spiritual topics. Given we had no romantic interests, this was a great conversation where Linda made clear a number of her expectations and standards.

Upon our return from our walk, we entered the house through the living room, where Jack, Bob, and some of the other guests there were gathered around a strange contraption in the center of the room emitting a funny odor. Linda and I went into the other room and were talking and looking at pictures. She asked what they were doing out there. I replied nonchalantly, "They're smoking pot in a bong."

Aghast, Linda refused to ever come back to the house and began to strongly encourage me to seek new roommates. She also started taking me before the Lord in earnest, and she convinced several prayer warriors at the Santa Clara Church to join her in praying for my exit out of this den of iniquity—fast!

As I began to regularly attend Santa Clara Church and became involved with the youth group, I grew increasingly convicted about my other six-days-of-the-week lifestyle. You see, the UCC church I grew up in, as many of the mainline denominations of today have sadly become, was a pleasant place to be. The sermons made me feel good and generally encouraged me to live a better life. They held fine social events. Yet, while there are many fine Christians in these churches, it is far too easy to attend a church like this every week and never come to a true understanding of the gospel and make true change to one's life. This was certainly the case with my hometown church during my youth. It didn't emphasize teaching the gospel. It didn't confront me with the need to develop a personal relationship with Christ, or the consequences of sin, or the convicting work of the Holy Spirit. While I might have heard bits and pieces of the gospel message, I wasn't challenged to live a New Testament lifestyle.

Now as I began to see the gospel unfold in front of my eyes, I was aware that my lifestyle was increasingly far off the mark. While

I had believed myself to be a Christian and declared such to Linda and many others, I had no personal relationship with and faith in Jesus Christ.

In February 1980, Gary Fraley, the minister at Santa Clara at the time, gave a sermon using Revelation 3:15–16 as the text:

> I know your deeds, that you are neither cold nor hot. I wish you were either one or the other! So, because you are lukewarm—neither hot nor cold—I am about to spit you out of my mouth.

During that sermon, I felt as if Gary were speaking to only one person in the room that day—me. I was challenged and convicted. I could clearly see that my other-six-days-of-the-week lifestyle placed me in the lukewarm category at best. I was, as Revelation so boldly declared, ready to be spit out of the mouth of the Lord.

With this conviction upon my heart, I made that step of faith, claiming Jesus as my Lord and Savior, understanding and repenting of my sins, turning toward a new way of life, and finally being baptized through the waters symbolizing his death, burial, and resurrection. I became a new creation in him. February 1980 was my second birth, my spiritual birthday. All of a sudden a new life and lifestyle began to powerfully unfold in front of me.

About a week later, I was casually walking down the hallway in Intel's Santa Clara 4 building. As I made a typical stroll on the way to the cafeteria, a short but fit man approached me. He was clean shaven, had short dark hair, wore glasses, and was probably around thirty years old. I had never met him before and didn't have any reason to believe he knew me. As he walked closer to me, he was clearly seeking my attention and apparently wanting to have a discreet conversation. "Greetings, I'm Bob Matthews," he declared in a clear and pronounced voice. We shook hands, and I was struck by his politeness and expected him to discuss some work-related topic. But then he quickly declared that God had informed him that he and I were supposed to be roommates.

I was shocked. God spoke to him about me? How bizarre! As a baby Christian, I was most unprepared for this. While peculiar and unnerving, it was also clear that my current rock 'n' roll and neo-Nazi roommates did not contribute to the spiritual environment I needed. Bob was a mature Christian, a quiet and helpful man, and just about perfect for me at the time. This leading from God was an example of his personally directing my life. As I was working and going to school and spending most every free moment in study, God had—in another of those divine coincidences—provided the perfect roommate.

The prayers of Linda and the other prayer warriors from Santa Clara Christian Church were answered; God provided a new roommate and a spiritually encouraging environment. With my newfound faith in the Lord Jesus Christ, the first of the great changes in my life in California was well under way.

SCHOOL

My hiring manager and first boss at Intel was David A. Brown. David took me under his wing, and I began as his technician in the Quality and Assurance group of the microprocessor department.

On my first day of work, Dave explained the things he needed me to do. He was running a variety of quality and reliability experiments and he needed me to load chips into ovens, run some tests on them at periodic intervals, verify the functioning of the test board and its load of chips, and then reload them into the ovens for additional stresses and tests. While not the entirety of my responsibilities, this was a large part of my starting assignment.

As I sat there listening to him, my singular career goal quickly congealed in my mind that very first day on the job—I wanted to be on the other side of the table. I wanted to be the one deciding the experiments, interpreting the data, and giving the direction. I wanted to be the engineer who decided what to do, not the technician who did the grunt work.

From this humble beginning, my career seed was planted. I spent all my spare hours working. I loved it. Compared to the farm, this was great. It was clean and air-conditioned compared to a hot and dusty day in the hay mound. There were no animals trying to kick or bite me. I even got paid for overtime!

When I wasn't busy with school, I'd easily work eighty or ninety hours in a week, often breaking the bank on overtime pay for our department. A couple of times my overtime was so extensive that payroll complained. I just told them to pay me for whatever number of hours didn't cause a problem.

One of the main reasons I had accepted a position with Intel was to continue my education. Now, it was quickly becoming clear that I wanted to be an engineer and proceed to graduate-level studies as well. Of the many job offers I had received, Intel offered me by far the most flexible work schedule. Further, Intel had a tuition-reimbursement policy: Any full-time employee (defined as anyone working thirty or more hours per week) who took a work-related course and received a grade of B or better would be fully reimbursed by the company.

With this policy and an agreement from my boss to allow me flexible work hours, I began my full-time studies at Santa Clara University in March 1980. I continued diligently for three years to complete my BS in electrical engineering. Then I immediately enrolled at Stanford University, where I earned my master's in June 1985. Following that, I spent another year getting started on my PhD at Stanford. Based on Intel's tuition-reimbursement policy, I was on my way to achieving the cheapest expensive education one could ever have. (Though I stopped attending school almost twenty years ago, I believe I still hold the record for the amount of tuition reimbursement provided by Intel to any individual employee.)

Having come from a small technical school on the East Coast, I was somewhat intimidated in my first quarter at Santa Clara University. Everyone here was smarter than anything I'd experienced before. I was nervous knowing that if I didn't get a B or better, Intel wasn't going to reimburse me. I moved to California with just a few dollars to my name, and not having earned enough in my first few months at Intel, I didn't have much of a financial cushion. I couldn't have afforded to pay for the classes I was taking.

This motivated me to labor hard to earn good grades, studying every spare moment of my nights and weekends. After the first quarter, I was getting As in all my classes, and I realized that with hard work I had a shot at being the top of the class. Thus, while it required great focus and increased diligence, I made up my mind to become class valedictorian.

With school and my career at Intel moving ahead, the second of the great changes of my life in California was in full swing. I was on my way to becoming an engineer!

LINDA

Having just moved to California in October 1979, I had neither funds nor vacation time for a trip home when Christmas came just a couple of months later. For this particular Christmas, Linda's father was uncharacteristically out of town. Thus, Linda and her family had a major hole in their normal Christmas plans. They decided to take pity on this poor lonely boy from Pennsylvania.

I was invited to join Linda, her mother, Shirley, and her grandmother for a Christmas Eve meal. A bachelor far from home is seldom known to turn down a free meal, particularly when three generations of fine cooks were sharing the kitchen for a Christmas feast! Even though I wasn't all that interested in young Linda Sue at the time, the least that would happen was that I wouldn't be quite so lonely, and I'd scarf a good meal in the process.

The evening surpassed everyone's expectations. We enjoyed a fine meal and good conversation, and played a variety of games. I hit it off extremely well with Linda's grandmother. As we played cards, it seemed we had something akin to mental telepathy working between us. The evening was wonderful, but I eventually made a graceful departure for my apartment.

As Linda's grandmother closed the door behind me that evening, she immediately turned and looked Linda in the eye. With generations of godly wisdom she declared to Linda and Shirley: "He's the one."

Linda not only disagreed, but she was shocked by the suggestion. "Grandma, he's just eighteen years old," she protested. "I don't know him, and he's just a friend!" She then proceeded to describe with great conviction my numerous other shortcomings in a futile attempt to convince Grandma of the erroneous nature of her statement! Despite Linda's objections, Grandma Christensen was firm in her prophetic assertion. Linda had great respect for her godly grandmother and, almost, a fear that Grandma saw something that Linda herself couldn't.

As Linda and I began seeing each other (casually but more regularly), her mother added to Linda's angst by reinforcing Grandma's opinion with her own: "He's the one." With both Mom and Grandma now firmly in my corner and rooting for me, you'd think I was certain to win over Linda. It just took her about two more years to be convinced!

As we began dating a couple of months after that Christmas Eve meal, Linda quickly learned how my life was prioritized and organized. Between Intel and school I fit her in each Friday night for our date night. I needed a break from studies and work, and Friday night was it. Further, she almost always cooked me a fine Friday-night dinner at her apartment. She would question, "Why don't we go out to eat?" To which I'd reply, "But I love your home-cooked meals!" She could never quite tell if I was honest about her cooking or just too cheap to take her out to eat. Both were true.

In addition to our Friday-night dates, we'd see each other on

Sundays at church. She would often cook a meal for us on Sunday afternoon after church. Then I'd hunch over my books at her apartment for several hours of studying while Linda would often curl up for a treat she'd look forward to all week—a Sunday-afternoon nap. We'd then venture off to Sunday-evening church service before bidding each other farewell until the next weekend.

While we never saw each other during the other days of the week, I'd call her almost every day for a conversation. Often the calls were nothing more than "Don't have time but wanted to check in and make sure you knew I was thinking of you." Years later we would joke about this period, saying, "We squeezed a year's worth of dating into three years."

On one occasion, Linda called me on Thursday and asked if we could get together. She'd had a disagreement and wanted someone to talk to. Being the flexible and nice guy I was, I said sure—no exams tomorrow, no assignments due, and no deadlines for anything at work. I spent a fair amount of time that evening discussing the situation with her. After awhile together, she was feeling much better.

As I left her apartment that night, Linda asked me with great anticipation what we would do the following night, Friday night, our normal date night. I immediately responded, "Sorry, you had your night. I have to study tomorrow." She was shocked, angry, and terribly disappointed with me. All her girlfriends were seeing their boyfriends four, five, or six days of the week, and now I was depriving her of the one night of the week I could squeak out for her. No date night! How could I be so callous and cruel? This led her to question if she could ever marry a guy like me. Would I ever change? Or would I always be so busy that I would never have time to fit her into my already full life? At a minimum, she'd think twice before asking for my time on a different night of the week! Today we can both look back on this situation and laugh. Now I clearly see my priorities were quite skewed, and I'd have clearly enjoyed a date that Friday night! Slowly, Linda has worked on me, and God has softened my heart to understand just how important relationships are in life. As the years have matured me, relationships are far more important than my self-imposed goals or deadlines. Fortunately, Linda was patient enough to work with me through my youth and zealous pursuits.

While I was becoming increasingly fond of Linda, I had also made my intentions abundantly clear to her. I was on the slow boat to matrimony. I was determined to finish my bachelor's, master's, PhD, and maybe even a bit of post-doc work before settling down to marriage and family. While she might not have liked my goals, she didn't press the issue with me. She respected my ambition and was reluctant to express any of her desires in our still-young relationship. Then, however, God began to work again.

For many years, Linda had been struggling with a disease—endometriosis—that had severely deteriorated her reproductive organs. A year and a half after we began dating, she had a surgery to correct some of the damage done by the disease. She had many cysts that had grown on her ovaries, tubes, and uterus. The doctor had to remove one ovary entirely. A portion of the second ovary had to be removed as well. Following the surgery, her gynecologist asked her if she was considering marriage ... engagement ... or maybe a boyfriend, making it very clear to Linda that if she was ever to have any children, it needed to be soon—very soon. Despite Linda's reluctance, her doctor insisted that she needed to discuss her medical condition with her boyfriend.

So in June 1981 Linda had me come to her apartment, which was a bit atypical. She made clear to me ahead of time that she had some things she needed to discuss with me. By the tone in her voice I knew it was rather ominous and that she was most uncomfortable with whatever the topic was. When she came out with a foot-high stack of medical books, I knew I was in serious trouble. As she opened them up to the reproductive section, I had an eerie premonition. I was pretty certain I wasn't ready for whatever she was about to share.

She began explaining to me everything the surgery had done and everything the doctor had said to her. I was overwhelmed and confused. School was going well. I was nicely maturing in my infant Christian faith. Work was great. I was enjoying this casual dating relationship with Linda. But, now …

My mind buzzed with each word as she pointed to various pictures. She was trying her best not to lose her composure as she systematically gave me the explanations of what the doctor and her own studies had brought her to understand about her condition. When she made the point about children now or never, it stung like being hit with ice-cold water while in a warm shower.

After she finished, I not only felt confused but trapped as well. At this point, I had probably fallen in love with her. How could I deprive her of any hope of natural motherhood? Should I simply break off the relationship and wish her well in finding someone who didn't have such firm and clear goals as I did—someone who wasn't on the slow road to matrimony? I needed to think, pray, and consider what we'd discussed.

Thus, partially out of fear and motivated to just get away from the immediate conversation, I told her I'd give her an answer before school began in the fall. With that, we concluded the conversation, and I was more than anxious to get out of there. Marriage? Pregnancy? Children? I wanted a large family, maybe eight or twelve kids—but certainly not now. What was God trying to tell me?

With a deadline set, I struggled all summer over this matter. We continued dating, but she could tell I was very troubled. Our times together were often just miserable. We spent a weekend camping with some dear friends, Joe and Kathy. As my school and work schedule was so busy, this was a good time to think about and consider our relationship. It proved to be a wretched weekend, however, as Linda lived in constant fear that at any moment I'd blurt out that I wanted out of the relationship.

After months of pondering and prayer, I did reach a decision. The very last weekend before school started, I took her out to eat (and it wasn't even a Friday night!). Since I was pretty much a tightwad, taking her to her favorite fish restaurant was a pretty big deal.

I encouraged her to pick anything at all from the menu she wanted. From Mr. Tightwad to Mr. Generous-and-Bighearted. She knew something was up. By this point, her stomach was tied in such knots that she could barely eat anything at all. Still being very much a frugal bachelor with no apparent care in the world, I ate all my dinner and most of hers as well.

When we went to my apartment after dinner, I had a dozen red roses awaiting her. Then, having finally listened to God's leading, I asked if she would be mine. With tears filling her eyes, she found the words and voice to say a clear and strong yes.

My struggle all summer was not an atypical one for many of us: our plans and desires, or God's? Are we willing to subjugate our plans to his clear will for our lives? For me it was a crisis of belief and direction. Often throughout Scripture we see this same sequence over and over again: Moses had a plan to save his people in Egypt, but God's plan was very different. God's plan to promote Joseph to leadership differed greatly from the path Joseph envisioned. Over and over through Scripture we see God's plan being different from our paths. His ways are not our ways.

While I couldn't anticipate at the time how great a complement Linda would be for me, she certainly was and is God's perfect choice. As the years have progressed, I've been continually thrilled to see her open up like a rose in front of me, each petal holding another character quality or personality attribute that I had not known she possessed before.

Where I'm extremely logical, Linda is emotional. While I might see the physical needs of the situation, she is sensitive to the emotional needs. I tend to be a maniac, forever trying to squeeze more into every week or day or hour. She understands how to rest and relax and acts like brakes on me, preventing me from spiraling out of control. Where I tend to react quickly and sometimes impulsively, she is much more methodical and practical. While leaving some things gray and ambiguous is just fine with me, she needs them to be perfectly black or white and insists on the highest clarity and integrity in everything. Being on time for me is plus or usually minus ten or fifteen minutes. For Linda, anything less than five minutes early is already being late. While I might be lax with what the kids watch or do, she is thorough, assuring our children are raised in an absolutely Christian and moral environment at all times.

While her doctor recommended marriage and pregnancy as quickly as possible, we decided to wait till the following summer to wed. We would plan it carefully, invite our relatives, and go through premarriage counseling at our church. While we were ready to wed and begin our family, we trusted that if God would give us children, he'd still provide them to us if we trusted him.

As we approached our wedding day in August 1982, her doctor realized she hadn't been inoculated for Rubella. After receiving the shot right before the wedding, she wasn't to become pregnant for three months. At precisely three months of marriage, that remaining portion of her single ovary and her tattered reproductive organs conceived our first child. When she went to see her doctor, they both cried. The doctor said, "I can't believe it since I know what you look like inside!" Remembering the barren womb of Elizabeth and her husband, Zechariah, the parents of John the Baptist, we named our first child Elizabeth. Just as God had blessed Elizabeth and Zechariah with a miraculous pregnancy, so he had blessed us with a pregnancy that even Linda's doctor considered a miracle.

August 1982 was the summer before my senior year at Santa Clara University. I still had another year there and then grad school. Still being focused on my goal of being top of my class, I either hunkered over my desk each evening while studying away, worked late at Intel, or attended classes. I also studied all weekend long most every weekend. While some might have thought the situation was terrible, Linda thought it was great. Instead of seeing me only on Friday night and at church on Sunday, she was seeing me every day and night! Even if she heard only a few words from me and watched me lean over my desk with my nose in a pile of technical books, we were at least together—every single day of the week!

I've counseled others over the years who are working and going to school to just "get it done" like I did. Trying to do a full-time job and go to school at the same time is, at best, a very challenging task. In retrospect I realize that I was a bit too maniacal about it. I certainly could have taken a bit more time for Linda along the way; more focus on our relationship would have been good for both of us. That is now my advice to others.

· · · · ·

Imagine a juggler spinning three small plates. One of those plates represents God, one represents family, and the third represents work. That's what my life felt like; I was constantly trying to keep all those plates in motion. I had no opportunity to pause, rest, or take a break. If I tired for a split second, one or more of the plates would crash to the ground.

Is that an accurate picture of what your life feels like? Can you relate to the picture of the juggler? If so, read on.

While there were some pain and struggles over the next several years, that tattered womb of Linda's conceived a second, a third, and then a fourth time. Elizabeth is now twenty-four. She completed her bachelor's degree in education and taught elementary school for two years. She is now attending George Fox University in Oregon in pursuit of her master's degree in education. She has grown into an incredible young lady who is both mature and committed to her faith. In the fall, she will be taking a position in Shanghai, China. I'm confident that God will use her in incredible ways as a schoolteacher over the coming years.

Following her is our first son, Josiah. When I found out it was "A boy!" everyone in earshot knew it. I was thrilled to have a son: someone to play and wrestle and just do boy things with! He is intelligent and quick-witted. He loves to play soccer and has played on a team every year since he was four years old. I was excited to study each of our kids when they were young to try to predict what they would like: what classes they might be good at, what sports they might like, what musical instrument they might play. Josiah was the most difficult for me to understand, being quieter and inward with his thoughts and feelings. Now twenty-one, he astonished me when he said he wanted to become a youth minister. He graduated from William Jessup University this year and immediately began as a youth minister at a church in California!

Following him was another son, Nathan, who is now nineteen. He has boundless energy and excitement and an overwhelming joy and passion for life. He stayed on Mom's lap for what seemed like two or three days before running off. He had two modes as a child: active, loud, and energetic—or … asleep! He loves to be heard and greatly enjoys playing the guitar. He decided in his midteens that he felt God was calling him into ministry. He just completed his second year at William Jessup University where he is studying music, worship, and youth ministry. We're anxious to see how God will use him in ministry someday!

Finally, that tattered womb brought forth our fourth and final child, our third son, Micah. Micah is the picture of a last child. He's tough and determined. He will argue about anything with you, being certain he's right or has a better understanding of the situation than you. While he's talked about mission work, maybe to Africa, he is now a bit uncertain as to exactly what path he wants to take in life, which is common for children as they cross from their senior year of high school into college life. He has the determination and skills that we're certain God will use in powerful ways.

As Psalm 127:3, 5 says, "[Children] are a heritage from the LORD.... Blessed is the man whose quiver is full of them." My quiver was filling up, and God's blessings were flowing mightily into my life. Isn't it amazing the things God Almighty can do when we put our trust in him and let him work in our lives? The third great change of my life after moving to California was our growing family.

Returning to that juggling picture for a second, I could now throw away the small saucer representing family and, with four kids, replace it with a salad plate. Spinning odd-sized plates of growing demands was definitely becoming more and more challenging.

INTEL

While Linda and school were well under way, my career at Intel was going better than I could have imagined.

In my job as a quality and assurance (Q+A) technician, I had an opportunity to do a little computer-programming work. My boss began teaching me how to program in the C programming language in my spare time, and he would give me a few modest work assignments to move me along in my programming skills. Between my boss's tutelage, taking programming classes at college, and my own self-learning, I was quickly acquiring this new skill. I also started to run the computer system of the Q+A department, which used the UNIX operating system.

I soon grew troubled by what seemed like an after-the-fact approach to quality and reliability at Intel. My thought was that rather than trying to test for quality *after* the chips were designed, maybe we could design reliability and test capabilities into the chips up front. Based on this notion and some support and encouragement from my boss, I started teaching myself about design and building test capabilities, and self-testing circuitry directly into the chip. This approach sounded logical, and there was a bit of work going on in the field, but most of it seemed pretty academic with only modest application to commercial-chip development. I began to engage with the chip design teams of the 80286. My hope was that I might get some of these ideas included in the 80386 design, which—with the 80286 coming to an end—was just about to get under way.

Intel had invented the microprocessor design in 1974. Others such as Motorola and National were jumping into this exciting new product area with designs of their own, though Intel remained the industry leader. Sometimes good, sometimes lucky—Intel had won the all-important IBM PC contract with our 8088/6 chip. The IBM PC was quickly proving to be "the design" that would redefine the entire industry. While the IBM PC was coming to the market later than other designs, it was not only a good design but also "open," meaning the internal specifications were made available to others for their own innovation and enhancement. This became a watershed event for the world of computing, and the design quickly ushered in the personal computer as we know and love it today.

IBM had relied on two critical pieces of external technology to quickly bring the PC to market: the microprocessor from Intel and the DOS operating system from Microsoft. Intel began to realize the strategic importance of this design win, and the company was beginning to align itself behind this strategic position. As a result, the best and the brightest in the company were part of the microprocessor design team.

Picture this with me: a twenty-year-old kid, who knew nothing about chip design, halfway through his bachelor's degree in electrical engineering, approaching the design team for *the* Intel microprocessor. While not quite holy ground, that team was probably as close as you could get at that time in the industry. They worked on the most important projects for the company and—as it turned out—the most important projects for the entire computer industry. Everything they did was recorded in the journals of the history of the industry. While I was somewhat intimidated, I didn't hesitate to approach the design team with some of these crazy designs for quality and built-in self-test ideas.

Naturally, the design team said, "Of course, we'll immediately implement your ideas. It's a shame we didn't think of them ourselves." Or not.

While my ideas weren't immediately rejected, they were greeted with more than a healthy dose of cynicism. However, while skeptical to the specific ideas I was proposing, the design team also saw this young, aggressive kid who might make a decent addition to the design team. Best of all, I knew UNIX.

This latter point, UNIX, turned out to be my ticket into the chip-design group. The 80386 team found these skills uniquely interesting and wanted me on the team. The design team was planning on moving off the corporate-supported CMS operating system to the more flexible and productive UNIX-based operating environment for their work. Thus, while the Q+A department sent me to the design group to get test capabilities built into the chip, the design team saw me as a chance to accelerate their rebellious move to a UNIX environment. The design team quickly sucked me in, and I was never to return to Q+A again.

After joining the design team, I cut my teeth on some wrap-up work for the 80286 design. Then, voilà, I was engineer number four on the 80386 design team! I was thrilled to be part of microprocessor development for Intel. I could never have dreamed of a position this exciting when I started working. I was learning by day and doing by night. Each day I was attending classes on various aspects of electrical engineering and computer science first at Santa Clara University for my bachelor's and then at Stanford for my master's degrees. At night I was actually designing the most important microprocessor chips in the industry.

I quickly moved through the design ranks, taking on increasing responsibilities in the chip project. A year after joining the 80386 design team, I began managing a couple of technicians who were doing schematics entry. I had wanted to be the engineer, telling the technician what to do, and I was excited about this new challenge of managing. I completed one block of the chip, the instruction decoding unit, well ahead of schedule. I was then given a second unit to design, the main data path. Completing this, I moved on to tackling even a third, the protection and test logic. I eventually was put in charge of the final assembly and "tapeout."

If you could compare tapeout to an airplane design, it's like the final assembly of the very first airplane. The wings, engines, fuselage, landing gear, and control systems are all independently designed by different subteams. Then we need to integrate each subsystem into a finished product. Tapeout is the equivalent for chips, bringing all the units together into a complete design for the first time.

After the tapeout is complete, the design is sent to the enormous and expensive silicon fabrication facilities. After three to four weeks, the first silicon wafers come back to the design team for "debug." Debug is sort of like starting up the engines of the plane, testing to see if the flight-control system really works, and checking whether the flaps and rudders operate correctly. Then comes the first test-flight: Can this thing really fly? If it has some problems, what are they? Where are the bugs and problems that our simulations didn't identify? Where did we make errors in the integration of the pieces into the whole? What changes are needed to get the chip working properly and ready to ramp into production?

The tapeout and debug process is extraordinarily visible to the company. After four years of laborious effort, mostly executed in relative solitude, now the world wants to know, does it work? The entire design team, the entire company, and hundreds of people at companies like IBM and Compaq are all anxious for updates and status, just like expectant parents, grandparents, and relatives for the birth of a first child. Needless to say, for someone of my age and level of experience, this was a huge level of responsibility.

This period was incredibly busy, intense, and exhilarating. While the first chips "worked," they had some problems. We would quickly fix those problems so we could continue to explore the chip and run more tests and software on it. We'd then identify more problems, for which we'd quickly work to do additional fixes. This cycle continued in rapid succession for several months. Following this period of just getting it to work, we gradually shifted to focus on making it manufacturable. Why were some chips good and others failing? What were the marginalities in the design, and how could we fix each of these as well?

As we completed the tapeout and debug phases of the 80386 and it moved toward full production, I was pulled off to start the 80486 design as the original designer and architect. Wow, employee number one on the next generation of the most important family of microprocessors on the planet! I labored on this for a year as well as some other tasks in development methodologies along with some cleanup work on the 80386.

However, having finished my master's degree from Stanford and continuing to receive encouragement from my parents, I was determined to complete my PhD. Thus, Intel unexpectedly received my resignation as I planned to continue my education full time. However, Andy Grove inserted himself and instead of letting me walk out the door, he challenged me, "Do you want to learn to fly the jet on the simulator or the real thing?" He was offering me the position of 80486 design manager! Imagine this, the crown jewel of Intel, the most important chip project in the industry, and I—having just finished my master's, a whopping twenty-five years old, and much less experienced than many of the people who would be working for me—was being offered the chance to run the whole project. I was flattered but also somewhat overwhelmed with the magnitude of the challenge and responsibilities. Needless to say, I abandoned the PhD dream and opted instead to "fly the real jet." I was challenged, working incredibly hard but also enjoying myself beyond measure.

Following the 80386 and 80486 projects and over the ensuing years, my career has continued to progress rapidly. For fifteen years, I received a promotion every year. I moved through being the design manager of the 80486, the 486DX2, and the Pentium Pro. All these chips carried the company and the industry for their period of significance and leadership. I became the general manager of our Internet, video-conferencing, and communications products, initiating many of the key technologies that have made the Internet a broad replacement for traditional switched-voice telephony.

I was given the honor of being promoted to vice president at the age of thirty-two, the youngest in the history of the company. I took on the mammoth assignment of being the general manager of desktop products, the largest business unit of the company, representing tens of billions in revenue. At thirty-five I became a corporate officer and joined the executive staff, the highest management body at Intel.

In the fall of 2001, I was promoted to be the first-ever chief technology officer (CTO) for Intel Corporation at the ripe old age of forty. Imagine the honor of being the CTO for one of the most technologically significant companies of the last fifty years. Imagine being the CTO of a company with leaders at its helm like Gordon Moore, Andy Grove, and Robert Noyce—legends in the industry. While they were the primary technical drivers of the company for many years, I was the first person ever to have received the title of CTO. I remember calling my mom up to inform her that it would be announced the following week that I was being promoted to be Intel's first-ever CTO. Mom replied, "That's great, honey. Now what's a CTO?"

Since then I have also been promoted to senior vice president of the Digital Enterprise Group. Currently I'm in charge of the largest business group at Intel, where I'm expected to provide both technical and business leadership. I've been so blessed that it's simply overwhelming.

Of course, while God's hand has been mightily upon me, I also have to pause and give great recognition to my employer, Intel. How many companies are truly merit based in their decisions on promotions and assignments? How many employers would take the risk of putting a twenty-five-year-old kid in charge of the crown jewels of the corporation's future? Over and over, Intel has given me opportunities, challenges, and rewards of tremendous degree.

At this point, though, let's return to the imagery of the juggler spinning plates. One small saucer was for work, another was for God, and we had already graduated to a salad plate for family. Well, throw away the saucer for work; it was now the size of a dinner plate!

CHURCH

Though family, school, and work take most of my time, Linda and I have always remained active in our local congregation. We began a Bible study in our home, and, except for the year we moved from California to Oregon, we have continued this practice for almost twenty years. We've found this to be a great blessing, an opportunity to share our faith with others and build many long-term relationships.

As our children go out on their own, I can only hope they will recall this example and find or host study and fellowship groups of their own. Unfortunately my work schedule now has me away too many weeknights; thus, we've not been leading a study in most recent years and instead have been participating in a small group on weekends.

You'll see a bit later in my personal mission statement that I put down as a goal to "become an elder in my local congregation." When I wrote that, I expected I would fulfill that when I was old and wise … maybe age fifty or sixty. However, writing a goal like that can be a little dangerous. When our minister preached a sermon on what biblical eldership was all about and the need for men to take roles of leadership in their families and their churches, I was pierced to the heart. While I remained silent, I knew well what was coming. I had written these goals years before and now felt God's moving in my heart. A few months later, I was called to be an elder. I served for eight years at Singing Hills Christian Church in Hillsboro, Oregon, and in particular helped through some challenging leadership transitions at the church.

As we'll discuss later when we cover tithing, Linda and I believe you should give more than just money, but also your time and talents to ministries you support. Thus, I've found myself currently serving as the Foundation Chair for William Jessup University and as an active consultant to several other ministries.

· · · · ·

If you hadn't guessed yet, I'm a busy guy. Furthermore, I enjoy being active, busy, and getting things done. Busyness and challenges get my adrenaline going. When I die, I want to be used up for God, having given everything I can to do my best for his kingdom. I never want to retire. In fact, I would challenge anyone to show where God suggests that people should retire. Passages like Philippians 3:14, 1 Corinthians 9:24–26, and Galatians 2:2 create a picture of a marathon runner going the whole distance and running hard to the finish line—graduation to the heavenly kingdom at the end of one's life on earth. So I simply want to move from one type of job to another as God leads. At some point along the way, I may stop working at a secular position, but it won't be for lack of ministry and work that I'm entirely involved in and consumed by.

Before bringing this chapter to a close, I'd like to go back one last time to that picture of a juggler spinning plates: salad plate for family, a dinner plate for work, and a saucer for God. Well, by this time, the kids have hit the teenage years, so throw the salad plate away for family. Those teenagers are now a bit odd, and they are better represented by an odd-shaped serving platter with very unpredictable and often extreme demands for time and attention. So, start spinning:

- a saucer for God,
- a serving platter for family,
- and a dinner plate for work.

Juggling is hard enough under the best of circumstances, but if you throw in some odd shapes and larger items, it gets really hard. Can you relate to this kind of experience and picture? If so, the following seven chapters of proven and practical advice should help you to manage better.

• • • • •

CHAPTER 1 QUESTIONS

Note: My own responses to these questions can be found near the end of this book.

1. Many people would argue that the Internet is evil. What do you believe about it and other technologies that have been used in questionable manners?

2. Chester Carlson, the founder of Xerox, attributed his sustenance during difficult times to the *Bhagavad Gita*, a Hindu spiritual text. Do you think that being spiritual is important, whether you are a Christian, Hindu, or Muslim?

3. In your time with God, do you ask him for help with your work or profession? Does God provide ideas, witty inventions, or specific help in the workplace? Do you have some ways to know how to proceed, such as what direction to take in your work?

4. Maybe you feel like you are working as hard as you can just to keep pace; you aren't a type-A overachiever and regularly need more sleep than Pat does. How do you achieve balance in life even though you consider yourself a more "normal" person?

5. How do you know if you are in the right profession? Could a struggle with balance occur because you are doing the wrong thing?

2

. . . . .

Developing a
Blueprint for Life

. . . . .

IMAGINE THAT TOMORROW MORNING, without warning, you loudly announce to all the members of your family, "We're going to leave today on vacation. Get ready to go right now!"

Of course, having no forewarning, your kids and spouse are a bit startled and start asking some straightforward questions like "Where are we going?"

To which you respond, "I don't know."

"What are we going to do?"

You say, "I don't know, we'll figure it out when we get started."

"How are we going to get there?"

You respond, "Not sure, but we'll get started and decide the rest as we go." After a few bewildered looks, you demand, "Pack your things, we're leaving in fifteen minutes."

To which your kids, now even more perplexed, reply, "How can we pack? We don't know where we are going. What should we take?

We don't know what we're going to do. How many days are we going to be gone?"

You say, "I'm not sure about any of that, but grab whatever you want for vacation and let's go. We're leaving in fourteen minutes!"

Of course, this is an unreasonable scenario. You don't just up and leave on vacation without any planning at all. You always have at least some sort of itinerary in mind, even when you're trying to be flexible and spontaneous. Is it a driving vacation, or are you flying somewhere? Are you going camping, or on a weeklong cruise? Are you going for just a day or two, or a couple of weeks?

I have a good friend who appears to live for vacations. Every time I talk with him, he's telling me about this rafting trip, that hunting outing, or a ski trip he has planned for a year or even two or three in the future. His vacation plans consume the majority of his discretionary time.

All of us will spend significant time and energy planning for a vacation. We'll develop an itinerary, purchase tickets, and make reservations. Likewise with major purchases like a car or a home, or decisions like choosing a child's college, we'll do thorough research and enlist the help and advice of others, and sometimes even get assistance from professionals such as architects, travel agents, or school counselors. At work, if given a big assignment by the boss, we'll plan every aspect of the job in detail. We'll develop schedules and budgets and resource plans till every detail of the project is completely understood.

So what's the point? While most of us will spend considerable energy planning in other areas, far too few of us have seriously considered and planned our most critical assets and the most limited resource we have: our gifts and our time. Do you have a destination in mind for your life? Do you have a strategy for how you are going to get there? How will you know when you've hit a critical milestone or when you have fallen off course? What do you want to accomplish with the rest of your life?

When I hit about thirty-two years of age, I began to sense some aimlessness and confusion. After moving to California in 1979 to start my career at Intel, I quickly developed a set of goals I wanted to accomplish. I just hadn't developed them formally or written them down, but I had a pretty clear set of things in my mind I wanted to accomplish. The problem was that, at thirty-two, I had already accomplished almost everything I had set out to:

- I had wanted to become an engineer, and I reached that goal with my promotion to engineer after joining the design team of the 80386 computer chip in 1982.
- After getting married—and given Linda's medical condition—we had a goal to start a family. Linda desired two children; I was more aggressive and said eight. We compromised and settled on four.
- I wanted to complete my education, and I got my bachelor's from Santa Clara in 1983, finished my master's from Stanford in 1985, and decided against attempting to finish a PhD.
- I had always wanted to be an inventor. I received my first patent on April 12, 1988, for the "Optimally Partitioned Regenerative Carry Lookahead Adder." (Fascinated, aren't you?)
- After finishing school, and with at least some discretionary time freed up, I began writing a book with the architect of the 80386, John Crawford. Finishing a book became another goal, and *Programming the 80386* was published by Sybex in 1987. I was an author!

- I wanted to move to a more family-oriented location to raise our kids. Oregon fit the bill nicely, and in 1990, we relocated to Beaverton, Oregon.
- I wanted to complete some significant projects at Intel, things I could forever look back on as my accomplishments. Having played a significant role in developing two of the most important chip projects in the industry, the 80386 and 80486 microprocessors, that goal was completed as well.
- I also wanted to increase my role and relevance at Intel, and I became the youngest VP in the history of the company at thirty-two years of age.

All of a sudden, I found myself struggling with the question of what I wanted to do with the rest of my life. What *else* did I want to accomplish? I felt as if the rudder had been taken off my ship and now I was wandering somewhat aimlessly, uncertain exactly where I wanted to go for the rest of my life.

DEVELOPING A PERSONAL MISSION STATEMENT

Through some reading, I stumbled onto the idea of writing a personal mission statement. Now that might sound easy, but for me and most everyone I've talked to, it's quite a difficult task. It requires arduous self-reflection and prayer. You need to think deeply about who you are, who you want to be, and what you want to accomplish with your life. It isn't something you just jot down on a napkin over lunch. I struggled to finish mine for over a year. I wrote drafts and then threw them away. Wrote them again and filed them away. Pulled them out a few months later and revised them, over and over. After a year of pondering and revisions, I had a version that I was pretty happy with and has stood the test of time since then.

You might ask, how does this process square with the familiar instruction found in James 4:13–15? Here's what the passage says:

> Now listen, you who say, "Today or tomorrow we will go to this or that city, spend a year there, carry on business and make money." Why, you do not even know what will happen tomorrow. What is your life? You are a mist that appears for a little while and then vanishes. Instead, you ought to say, "If it is the Lord's will, we will live and do this or that."

While on the surface there seems to be conflict, I don't think there really is. God has placed into each of us a set of gifts and skills, often referred to as talents. Psalm 139:14–15 says each of us is "wonderfully made" and "curiously wrought" (KJV). Romans 12:6 tells us, "We have different gifts, according to the grace given us. If a man's gift is prophesying, let him use it in proportion to his faith."

God takes the unique creation of each individual and then extols the virtues of using our talents to do great things for the kingdom:

> "Well done, my good servant!" his master replied. "Because you have been trustworthy in a very small matter, take charge of ten cities." (Luke 19:17)

He even chastises those who choose to leave their talents unused:

Then he said to those standing by, "Take his mina away from him
and give it to the one who has ten minas." (Luke 19:24)

He praises those who create fruit for the kingdom:

This is to my Father's glory, that you bear much fruit, showing
yourselves to be my disciples. (John 15:8)

He encourages his followers to develop themselves and to seek
leadership in the church. He praises the craftsman, he considers
learning and knowledge a gift to be carefully utilized, and he extols
the woman of Proverbs 31 for her wisdom and planning. Thus, we
find plenty of support for the idea of developing a personal mission
statement in the Scriptures.

What do we make then of James 4? Instead of dissuading us
from planning our lives, I believe the passage addresses people who
ignore the certain eventual return of our Lord Jesus Christ—those
who try to live as if Jesus doesn't exist and are living their lives with
no regard for his eventual and certain return.

Thus, I believe strongly that the idea of writing a personal mission
statement can be a powerful activity. I've seen this be significant not
only in my life but in the lives of others who I've worked with over the
years in drafting their personal mission statements as well. With that
in mind, I offer up below an excerpted version of my personal mission
statement as an example you might find helpful in crafting your
own. I'd like to make clear that this is *my* mission statement. This is a

statement of who I am striving to be and what I want to accomplish. I'm still far from being this person and have a lot of work to do to complete a number of the items listed herein. *This isn't a statement of what I've done, but of what I aspire to become.* This isn't a picture of who I am but of what I believe God has created me to become.

Of course, a personal mission statement is exactly that: personal. My gifts and passions from God are different from yours. My bent is not your bent. Consider mine as possibly a template that might be somewhat helpful in crafting your own.

I would also challenge you that you must, as I had to, go through a period of soul-searching in developing your personal mission statement. This is hard work, and you wouldn't be giving the task justice by trying to get it finished over a single weekend or week. You may get something down on a piece of paper that quickly, but those goals will not likely pass the test of time or be the goals you are aspiring toward. This is a deep soul-searching exercise; plan on dwelling on your goals for a while, and when you're finished, you'll have something useful for many years to come.

Your goal should be a document that lasts ten or twenty years, and at the end of that period still has you striving to be better. Mine has lasted me almost fifteen years, and I'm still far from done with it.

After I completed mine, I made one round of edits to it a couple of years later and then periodically a few very minor modifications. I did a fair amount of "wordsmithing" when I wrote the first edition of this book, in particular adding Scripture references to each value to help better orient my value statements to be aligned with Scripture.

As the last of our kids is leaving the home, I'm starting to sense it will soon be time for a major revision as Linda and I enter the next phase, chapter, or epoch of our lives. As you move through the periods of early adulthood, family and child rearing, and into empty nesting and early grandparenthood, and then finally retirement or post-career years, each of these transitions probably defines a good point in time to think again carefully about your personal mission statement. When you are just beginning your family years, it might be hard to have a very precise and clear view of what you will want to do in empty nesting and when your children begin families of their own. Similarly, when you are just coming to the end of the child-rearing years, it may be difficult to fully comprehend what you'd consider goals and objectives when you are no longer working a more-than-full-time job and you have far more discretion as to how to spend your time and resources in the latter years of life.

A few other comments as you consider drafting your own personal mission statement: After you have a draft you like, ask your spouse to read it. Ask if this is the kind of person he or she thought they married and hopes you will become. While I firmly believe these are personal goals, you need to know if where you want to go with your life and where your spouse wants you to go are reasonably well aligned. If you find they are not, this exercise may be a great way to identify some long-term areas of conflict with your spouse that you haven't recognized before. If they are aligned, this is a good opportunity to gain your mate's support and encouragement for this lifelong, purpose-filled mission toward which you are now committing yourself.

I'd also suggest you have a small number of trusted friends or mentors (more on this in chapter 6) read your mission statement.

Ask if these goals are consistent with your character and personality as they see it from a different perspective. Their independent assessment of you is probably more valuable and insightful than you can fathom. You might find that input from other individuals close to you will help you get a different perspective on yourself. Maybe some of those goals you think you want to pursue really don't match the character that other people see in you.

MY PERSONAL MISSION STATEMENT

Mission: I will be a Christian husband, family man, and businessman. I will use every resource God provides me to carry out his work on earth as set forth below.

Values: The things I will stand for, my values I will be recognized for. I will:

1. Work hard in all that I do. (Col. 3:23)
2. Give my best effort in every task. (1 Thess. 4:1)
3. Be open to the direction of the Holy Spirit wherever that may lead. (John 14:26)
4. Enthusiastically approach new challenges and all else I do. (2 Cor. 9:2)
5. Live by Christian principles. In all things I will try to make Christ's ethics and morals my own. (Rom. 2:7–8)
6. Be open, honest, and generous. (2 Cor. 9:11)
7. Be careful with words and actions. (James 1:26)
8. Seek the counsel of others frequently and thoughtfully. (Prov. 15:22)

9. Never be satisfied with the status quo. I will be an agent of change. (Rom. 15:20)
10. Seek to improve and grow those around and beneath me in work and all other areas. (1 Thess. 5:14)
11. Not seek my own glory, I will seek to honor God and have praise be given to those around me. (Rom. 15:5–6)
12. Never take things too seriously but have a great time in everything, continually enjoying God's blessings. (James 4:13–15)

Goals: The things I will accomplish, my goals. I will:

1. Make my marriage an example of that laid out in the Scriptures. I will be a one-woman man seeking the growth of my wife. I will assist her in the duties of our household, date her regularly, and cherish her always.
2. Encourage all four of my children to make personal commitments of faith to Christ, publicly demonstrating their new life through baptism. Play an active role in leading them into Christian maturity.
3. Assist in bringing over one hundred people to Christ or to a much greater degree of Christian maturity.
4. Write a book explaining the things God has taught me throughout my life for my children, grandchildren, and great-grandchildren.
5. Generate substantial wealth for my employer.
6. Become president of Intel Corporation. I will do so while maintaining my values and ethics.
7. Be an elder of the congregation at which we worship.

8. Give an increasing portion of all I earn to charity: church, missions, and other Christian organizations.

9. Provide financially for my wife, children, and grandchildren.

10. Spend quality and quantity time with my children while they are young. On average, I will dedicate ten hours per week to personal time with them.

11. Visit over fifty foreign countries to develop a broad worldview and a passion for all of God's creation.

12. Assist other Christians to achieve success in their profession and careers.

13. Continually be in the Word of God. I will be in the Word on a daily basis. I will read the Bible through at least twice each year.

14. Memorize Scripture. I will add to my repertoire at least ten new verses each year.

15. Continue to read. I will read at least five significant books each year.

16. Continue to learn. I will pick up at least one new topic, sport, field, or craft per year.

17. Continue to teach. I will teach at least one class each year.

18. Become fluent in at least one additional language.

19. Fast one day per week for the spiritual health and protection of my family and children.

20. Exercise regularly, at least three times per week.

21. Lead weekly Bible study.

I found that developing the three sections worked very well. If you've read other works on this subject, they may or may not follow this type of structure. Use any format you like and on any material you like—papyrus, paper plates, or napkins included. The three sections have some utility:

Mission: A simple, short statement. If you were going to have your epitaph written tomorrow, what would you want it to say? If you can answer that, that's a good place to start. If not, it's time to start some serious self-examination. In my mission statement the two key words are "every resource." When my time on earth is complete, I want to be like Paul and have run the good race (2 Tim. 4:7). I want to have used up every ounce of energy, minute of time, dollar of finances, and any other resources I have for his purpose and kingdom.

Values: For me, these are the statements I want people to think of immediately when asked, "What's Pat like?" A few years ago, I was challenged on some behaviors I'd exhibited at Intel over the years and was pointedly asked if I thought people would consider them consistent with my Christian faith. I was prone to overstating my accomplishments while sometimes demeaning the work of others. I also would want to own and control topics and resources for which I should rather have been more appropriately a mere stakeholder or even a consultant. Sadly, I had to confess that, no, those behaviors were not consistent with my faith and the person I desire to become. I was cut to the heart, and I was prompted to strong personal corrective action.

Goals: Get specific enough that you can regularly measure your progress against these goals. Hopefully over many years you will accomplish some of these and be able to check them off as completed. Several might be continual, such as reading so many books per year or exercising so many times per week. Others will come and go as you reach certain milestones, such as baptizing your last child into a personal relationship with Christ or writing a book. A couple of comments on some of my goals:

Goal 4: *Write a book explaining the things God has taught me throughout my life for my children, grandchildren, and great-grandchildren.*

As I was encouraged to consider writing the book you are now reading by several who had heard my juggling talk, I came face-to-face with my personal mission statement. Without this written down as a clear goal, I don't think I'd have undertaken the work you are now reading. Also, as I wrote this goal many years ago, I wanted to pass on what I've learned to future generations of my offspring. As such, I've tried to make this a much more personal work than I would have otherwise. Several have commented after reading the first edition of the book that they feel like they have a personal relationship with me and my family. Now as I'm drafting the second edition, I hope to further give windows into the depth of my person, my family, and my heart.

Goal 7: *Be an elder of the congregation at which we worship.*

As noted above, given this was already on my mission statement, I couldn't ignore the request when I was asked to serve in this capacity. Without having written this some years earlier, I would have probably rationalized away the request, saying "sometime in the future." As we know, the future never really gets here. Thus, we need to set goals and priorities and then live by them. While God doesn't need us to write a mission statement for us to make ourselves available for ministry, as humans we are far too willing to dismiss his quiet voice in our lives. Having it written down and being ready to be accountable to others makes us far more willing to stop and ponder when the time comes.

Goal 9: *Provide financially for my wife, children, and grandchildren.*

This goal led Linda and I to develop wills and trusts for our children and ourselves almost fifteen years ago. About five years ago we entirely revised them, reflecting more of our current financial situation as well as looking forward to future generations. If you haven't yet written a will, I'd challenge you to do so. This is one of those things that is very easy to procrastinate. Right now, stop and take a specific step to get started. Write it in your planner, call up your attorney, or make a commitment with your spouse to get this done. In many states and countries, the lack of financial plans and wills may lead to substantial additional taxes, as well as to a much greater public disclosure of your financial status (or lack thereof). Proper financial planning, trusts, and wills can assure confidentiality is maintained while the maximum transfer of financial worth occurs to your family and charities and interests as you and your spouse desire.

• • • • •

Your goals might be radically different from mine. They might include buying a home, getting out of debt, going into the ministry, starting your own business, finding a Christian spouse, choosing and completing a degree, starting a new church, going on short- or long-term missions, adopting a child, achieving specific financial or family goals, and so on. Let your mind wander some, brainstorm more, and when you're done, your mission statement should be something that makes your passions swell.

After your mission statement is finished, come back and read it every month or two, or at least once per quarter year. Ask yourself if you've been making progress toward those values and goals. On most occasions when I read mine, I see an area I should be doing more, or I'll reflect on some actions or incidents where I failed to execute according to my values. I'll often decide on some additional actions I need to take toward a particular goal.

Generally, I find these readings uplifting as I'll see at least some areas of progress, and the passion of what I'm to become always encourages me forward. Sometimes, they can be depressing as well. Looking at a picture of what you want to become and seeing your inadequacies can be discouraging—particularly after a bad day, week, or month. I'd also suggest you occasionally give a new copy to your spouse or a close friend or mentor and ask, "Is this still the person you want me to become?"

Once a year, formally grade your progress toward your goals. I keep a spreadsheet in which I specifically grade each year how I did against each of the twenty-one goals noted above. How many books did I read, and what were the titles and authors? I write them down as an entry for that year under that particular goal. Did I meet my Scripture-reading and memory goals? For many years this was an area I wasn't consistently developing, though my goals had stated I would. I pull out the tax forms and calculate how well we did against our giving goals, and then I plan the appropriate giving objectives and specific giving plan for the next year for our family. I tend to do this "grading" at tax time in April. I already have all my financial information pulled together, and I'm already usually a bit depressed about all those taxes I've paid. Thus, I find this to be a good point for me to make sure I also do a formal grading of myself against my values and goals.

Praise the Lord, some of my goals are mostly completed, as is the case with goal 2. All four of my children have now accepted Christ as their Lord and Savior. Even though this goal is partially complete, I enjoy reflecting positively on it, and thus I haven't bothered to revise the overall list. Also, since the second half of this goal states, "Lead them into Christian maturity," it challenges me to continue to pray for them and bring them before the throne of God on a regular, if not daily, basis. It also inspires me to find ways to encourage them to remain strong in the faith and continue to live in a manner reflecting their decision to follow Christ. This might be nothing but a short question during a phone call—"How are you doing in your spiritual walk?"—or a dinner or evening discussion with a larger agenda to it.

At this point I would exhort you to do as the Nike slogan says: "Just Do It." I recently had lunch with a good friend who wanted to work on his priorities. Knowing of my teaching and book writing on this subject, he had asked for a copy of this manuscript. Our lunch meeting was several months later, and he had commented on several occasions in the interim how much he appreciated the manuscript and how helpful it was as he began his own journey of becoming a better juggler.

After we had discussed different items for a while, I asked him pointedly if in fact he had written down his personal mission statement. He sheepishly replied he hadn't. I was a bit taken aback. While he had given me all sorts of positive indications about the value of the book, he wasn't turning what he'd learned into specific actions for his life. He needed to start writing. I was discouraged that he wanted to "get together and talk," having not even taken seriously his need to do some soul-searching and work. I made it clear that before we would meet again, I expected him to have completed a substantive draft of his own mission statement. Thankfully, in subsequent meetings, he did arrive with a draft of his mission statement in hand. I critiqued his drafts several times to make them longer term and more aspirational. After several revisions, his mission statement is in pretty good shape—now on to the hard work of living up to it!

Likewise, I pray that you will use my personal mission statement to help you in developing your own and that the exercise will give you a stronger sense of purpose and direction for your life. You do not want to be living randomly from day to day, but with purpose for the rest of your life. A focused life has great power. I'd hope that at the conclusion of this process, you feel an increased sense of purpose and focus as you move toward intentional living.

DISCIPLINE

No discussion of mission, goals, and priorities could be complete without some discussion of personal discipline.

As Linda and I were dating, on more than one occasion she expressed disappointment with the amount of time I spent with her. She saw her friends getting a much bigger share of their boyfriends' time than she had of mine. In response, as mentioned earlier, I developed a detailed assessment of the time I spent on each activity during the week. I laid out on a twenty-four-hours-a-day, seven-days-a-week chart all the time that was to be dedicated to school, to studying, to work, to church, to chores, to sleep, to her, and to personal leisure; and after all of that, I indicated whatever was left over.

Then I reviewed the chart in detail with Linda. Her response was, "You don't have any more hours." In fact, at this period of my life I didn't; my schedule was completely full. I clearly understood where the hours were going, and they were aligned with my priorities at the time. While it was difficult, Linda understood and could accept the situation. In fact, while she wished for more time from me, she was always attracted to the discipline she saw in how I lived my life. In retrospect, I wish I had been a bit more flexible with my time and devotion to her, but it took years of wisdom to help me understand the value of relationships more clearly.

I recommend you do a detailed time study for yourself to see where you spend your time. Make an estimate of how many hours each week you take for the major activities of your life: work, school, rest, entertainment, hobbies, spouse, children, commuting, church, God, friends, and so on. Then, over a typical period of your life, take two weeks and do a detailed time study. Keep track of how you spend your time, using fifteen- to thirty-minute increments. After you have gathered the raw data, categorize them carefully into the major groups: rest, work/school, church/God, family, and recreation. Create subcategories as appropriate for anything that might consume multiple hours per week, like listing commuting under work or TV under recreation. Finally, with the summary in hand, make the difficult assessments about how you are using your time. Ask yourself:

- Any surprises? Areas where I just couldn't imagine I was wasting—er, uh, um, spending—so much of my time?
- Is this where I want my time to go?
- Am I putting as much time as I'd like into the areas I want as the priorities in my life?
- How much time am I really spending with my spouse? Children? Friends?
- Did I realize how much time I was spending at work?
- If I wanted to spend more time on XYZ or ABC, in what areas would I consciously choose to spend less time?

As you finish your personal mission statement, you'll probably end up with more goals than you have time to pursue. Where will those extra hours come from? A detailed time study can reveal hidden diamonds in your day. Do you really need to sleep that long or are you being just a bit lazy? If you wanted to, could you crawl out of bed a bit earlier on weekends and get in more physical exercise or time with your children? Is playing three rounds of golf each week really that important to you? Could some of those hours in front of the television be spent instead truly focused on your mate? In what part of your day or week could you chisel time into your schedule to be more consistent with your devotions?

In no way am I condemning any particular activity. Maybe building relationships on the golf course is absolutely consistent with your mission statement. It may be an important part of your job or career. Maybe it's not just rest but also time when you build relationships and mentor others. It may be the essence of your personal recreation time and time to be refreshed and renewed each week. Maybe you do want to spend a good amount of your leisure time watching sports on TV—great! I'm only challenging you to make these conscious decisions based on thoughtful consideration and planning. With far too many individuals that I've counseled and conferred with over the years who've taken the step of doing a personal time study, they were spending time not based on conscious priority but largely on events happening to them, habit, or inertia. I have yet to find the individual who said, "Yup, I'm using my time in harmony with my mission statement, and I wouldn't make trade-offs to be more intentional about how I live my life."

With my chaotic lifestyle and all the travel I do, including many meals in fine restaurants, I've found it hard to exercise and easy to put on unwanted pounds and inches. Thus, I set a goal of getting back to my marriage weight. I began getting into the habit of packing my running shoes and shorts for overnight trips and booking into hotels with good workout facilities. Using a few spare minutes here and there, making it a priority to get up early and work out, I've gotten myself into better shape than I'd enjoyed for the past twenty years. In this particular area, it's often good to have a buddy to whom you are accountable. I often play racquetball at the gym early in the morning. It might be easy to hit the snooze button for the treadmill, but knowing Ed is expecting me at the gym is just a bit harder to snooze through.

Don't finish all your corrective action plans just yet, though. Wait until you've finished a few more chapters. I have some more tools and priorities for you to consider before you compile your "action required" list.

Finally, I'd encourage you to redo your time study periodically. The first time I did this for myself, I was in school and my time was well structured and accounted for. While some of the categorized data was a bit startling, I was pretty much living by my priorities in that season of my life.

The second time I did the time study, the findings were more surprising. I was out of school, and my schedule had become more dynamic and much less structured. Thus, the results of this study had a much greater impact.

What I discovered was that having finished my master's degree meant there was more time available for Intel. Managing the 80486 project, with more than one hundred people reporting to me, gave me a huge sense of responsibility. Every mistake or problem became my personal mission. As the flight director said in the movie *Apollo 13*, "Failure is not an option." And I thought the surest way to prevent it was to work more hours.

The time study revealed I was routinely putting in more than eighty hours per week. My arrival time home kept getting later and later. I had again slipped out of balance. Seeing those results in black and white shouldn't have been a surprise—Linda had been sending all the signals I should have needed for months—but it was.

Over the years, each succeeding study has brought fewer surprises, but I've still been challenged to make changes to my activities every single time.

· · · · ·

This probably sounds like a lot of work, and frankly, it is. However, let's remember that our time is the most precious resource God gives us. We can't stop or even slow its passage, and we can't get more of it. Our time on earth is like a vapor that disappears quickly (James 4:14). But we can make conscious and specific decisions on how we use it. So, while getting a handle on it can be laborious, the alternative is to naively lose track of this priceless, nonrenewable resource.

· · · · ·

CHAPTER 2 QUESTIONS

1. Why do you really need to prepare a personal mission statement with specific values and goals?

2. What kinds of time-management tools do you use?

3. How can you set goals or mission statements when the world around us changes so fast?

4. How should you go about developing a will and detailed financial plan for your family?

5. If you haven't started writing your personal mission statement, do a first draft right now. Use the three-section example given in this chapter as a model. Share the results with your spouse, mentor, or close friend.

3

. . . . .

Prioritizing God

. . . . .

DURING ONE PARTICULARLY challenging week at Intel, I had a number of customer meetings to attend and several presentations to give. I felt especially anxious about a CSD (corporate strategic discussion) presentation I was to be making that week. The topic was highly contentious, it represented a substantial business risk for the company, and all the top management would be there—including the CEO, Gordon Moore, and the president, Andy Grove.

The only way to prepare to lead such a discussion is to put in a lot of time and effort. That meant several late-night working sessions for the team and me, and all this in addition to my normally heavy workload.

One result was that my personal devotional times went out the window that week. No feeding of my spirit, no laying of my burdens before the Lord in prayer. By the time the big presentation rolled around, I was exhausted, nervous, and way out of balance physically, emotionally, and spiritually.

Not surprisingly, the presentation didn't go very well. Though the team supported me well and some of my peers coached me to get me through the actual presentation, the strategy we proposed was considered weak and was challenged by Andy in particular. Beyond the poor presentation, I also felt tired and inadequate in carrying out the rest of my duties. By the end of the week I was kicking myself, knowing I'd had to relearn a lesson I never should have forgotten—make time daily for God. I've heard it said that "maturity is learning the lessons you thought you already knew."

I could put no single item more firmly in this category than the need to prioritize daily time with God. How often I've gotten myself mired in a long and dreadful day, struggling with issue after issue, feeling nothing could go right and seeing nothing but darker and more ominous clouds on the horizon. Somewhere in that ugly, hurried, and hazy fog of daily activities, I'll be pricked back to a spiritual consciousness and ask myself if I have been in God's Word that day. Have I had my daily devotions and prayer time? Have I left these issues and concerns at the throne of the Father? Have I sought his help and guidance throughout the day? Am I living with the Holy Spirit as my guide and comforter right now?

Time and again, the answer will be no, I haven't been in the Word or in prayer. Yet again, I had somehow gotten busy or self-centered enough that I decided that God isn't really capable of carrying or helping with these burdens. I can better handle them all by myself. Once again, as in that dreadful week at Intel, Paul's cries seem so appropriate:

> I do not understand what I do. For what I want to do I do not do,
> but what I hate I do. And if I do what I do not want to do, I agree

that the law is good. As it is, it is no longer I myself who do it, but it is sin living in me. I know that nothing good lives in me, that is, in my sinful nature. For I have the desire to do what is good, but I cannot carry it out. (Rom. 7:15–18)

How refreshing to come to the throne of the Father and be united with him in prayer and study of his Word. I've not sat down and kept statistics for good versus bad days, but I can assert with confidence that I handle the rough days and situations so much better if I've been in the Word and prepared myself for the day with my God and Father. How different a countenance I carry on those days when I've been to the throne room. My attitude is better, my patience more robust, my tongue more careful, my discernment greater, and my patience increased. This is especially true when I realize my real employer is not Intel, but rather my heavenly Lord and Father.

As I've had to struggle with this challenge over the years, I've tried to develop some little habits that help to bring to mind my daily devotion time.

During the period I was going to school and into the early part of my Intel career, if something wasn't technology related or directly applicable to school or work, I didn't bother with it. In fact, on one occasion, I was so focused that I wasn't even aware that the world was "blowing up." After Mount Saint Helens erupted on Tuesday, May 18, 1980, Linda and I were together for our regular Friday-night date. She mentioned something about the volcanic eruption, and I asked what she was talking about. It had been the largest eruption in recent history. The Northwest looked like a war zone, skies over much of the nation were clouded with volcanic ash, millions of acres of lush forest had evaporated in just a few minutes, and I didn't even know about it three days later.

Early in my time at Intel, Andy Grove challenged me to read daily the *Wall Street Journal*. I made it a habit, and over the twenty years since then I've read it more than 75 percent of the time. I started to see, though, that on occasion I would get in my *Wall Street Journal* time without getting in my Bible time. From this, I committed to never read the *Journal* prior to finishing my daily devotional time; I'll read God's Bible before reading the businessman's bible. This has created a natural reminder for me.

I wish I could report a perfect success record since I put this regimen into place. But sometimes I oversleep, other times I get too easily preoccupied with something I'm working on, and other times it turns out to be just a particularly difficult or busy week.

While each of us is different, I'd encourage you to find that habit or event that will encourage you to make time for personal devotions every day. Maybe you make a commitment to God that his Word and prayer come before coffee or breakfast in the morning. For those of us who love that morning cup of java, we'd not miss daily devotions very often! Maybe you'll decide to talk to God before you make your first work phone call of the day. Or perhaps your thought will be that you feed your spirit before feeding your body each day. Maybe that you will exercise your spiritual muscles before exercising your physical ones at the gym. If you're a night person, you might choose to lay your life before the Father before laying your body down to rest.

This latter one doesn't work for me. Trying to have devotions in bed after a long day will almost certainly find me in a long, deep, prayerlike trance called sleep! Whatever works for you—however you need to bribe yourself, encourage yourself, abuse yourself, or reward yourself—just do it. Find something that will prod your consciousness and remind your brain so that daily devotions become a daily habit.

When I travel, I often have my prayer time on the way to the airport. It's usually early in the morning and about a forty-minute drive. After grabbing my morning latte at my favorite coffee stand, I'll sing a few hymns or praise songs to start out with. I then pray through the "ACTS" acronym (a popular form of prayer) as I'm making the drive to the airport on the other side of town:

A.   **Acknowledgment**—Praising God for who he is, what he is, and what marvelous things he has done in my life. Specifically bringing to mind areas and ways I've seen him at work, and acknowledging him as the God, Father, Creator, and Savior.

C.   **Confession**—Specifically laying my sins before the throne. Yet again calling on the body and blood of the Savior to cleanse me from all unrighteousness. Praying for strength and wisdom to combat any areas of sin, temptation, or challenges I am having in my life.

T.   **Thanksgiving**—Thanking him for the numerous blessings he has given me. Specifically calling to mind family members and events of the day or week for which I am particularly thankful.

S.   **Supplication**—Making those specific requests that I have for the Father. I always pray for the daily needs of my wife and each of the children by name. I pray that each of the kids might be holy and pure before God; that they might be useful in their professions for him; that their future spouses are being set aside in holiness and purity for them; and that their future in-laws are holding their children up in prayer as I am mine. By the time our kids have married, thousands of prayers will have gone up to the Father for each one of them and their future spouses. I also pray for my church, minister, missionaries, and church elders, and, finally, the requests of my Bible-study group and other specific needs I've become aware of. I keep a little card in my Bible listing the specific individuals I'm committed to pray for on a regular basis.

Usually by the time I'm parking at work or at the airport, I'm about prayed out. When I get to my seat on the plane or the parking lot at work, I will whip out my Bible and read a chapter or two in the New Testament, a chapter or two in the Old, and then work on the verses I'm memorizing. If I'm flying, about the time the plane has reached the "10 minutes or 10,000 feet" announcement, my laptop comes up, and I work for the remainder of the flight.

I also recommend a regular routine of committing Scripture to memory. If you have any doubts about the Bible's view on memorization, read Psalm 119, particularly verse 11: "I have hidden your word in my heart that I might not sin against you."

Of course, there are numerous overused excuses for not memorizing Scripture: *I can't memorize. I don't have time. I do it and later forget them all. I'm too old.* Of course, while memorization is easier for some than others, we all know we really can memorize if we really want to. We know our house number, phone number, family, and friends just to name a few things. In just a few minutes a day you can start to build a repertoire of verses you can utilize for the entirety of your Christian walk.

Typically, I spend about five minutes at the end of my devotion time on memorization. I usually work on two to three verses at a time. I read them over several times, then try to do a few phrases from memory. Next, I try a few whole verses and so on. Often I'll try to find little hints in the passage, like taking the first letters of key words and using that sequence to help prompt my memory as I work through the passage. The next day, I'll come back and work on these verses again. I'll keep working on them until I have them mastered. Usually, in a week or two I'll have pretty well nailed down a few new verses.

Many of us have at some point in our spiritual walks memorized Scriptures and have now long ago forgotten them. Some of the classics like the Lord's Prayer or the Twenty-third Psalm are often part of those we'd have picked up somewhere along the way. The magic to building a scriptural memory bank is regular review and refreshing. After memorizing a new section of Scripture, I'll then spend the next several weeks reviewing all the passages I've already memorized.

Work your way through your entire portfolio of verses, taking time to review them all. Brush up on any trouble spots and keep them all fresh in your mind. After you've done so, start again with a couple of new verses. Work on that new passage for a period of time depending on how long it is and how quick you are with memorization. However, review is again the most important step, so you might also find other creative ways to do that. You might write the verses on index cards and review them at red lights while driving. Or you could print them in large type and review them while on your exercise machine. You might tape them to your bathroom mirror. Take those spare couple of minutes here and there, and use them to review and refresh your memory, and you'll soon have a collection of twenty, thirty, fifty, or more verses you've committed to memory.

I find this cycle of repeated review essential for building a repertoire and breaking the habit of learning and quickly forgetting. Of course, there is also the question of what verses to memorize. It's all God's Word, so none of it is bad. Generally, choose verses that speak especially powerfully to you. Choose passages that might be helpful in areas where you want to focus your spiritual growth. Finally, choose verses that can help you battle specific areas of sin. Just to help you start, you might begin with verses that are already familiar to you. I'd also encourage you to pick one translation and stick to it.

My current repertoire is listed here. Maybe you'll find some of these you would like to add to your own: Job 31:1; Psalm 23:1–6; Micah 6:6–8; Matthew 5:1–16; John 1:1–18; Romans 3:21–24; 12:1–2; Phil 4:6–9; Colossians 3:1–13; 3:23–24; 1 Corinthians 13; 1 Peter 1:1–9; 2 Peter 1:5–11; and Revelation 3:15–16; 21:1–7.

• • • • •

A few years ago I was going to speak at a "Timeout" conference. However, my flight out of Portland was delayed due to a low cloud ceiling in San Francisco. We had the opportunity to circle for half an hour as air traffic was slowed and just one runway was in use. By the time we were finally given clearance to land, despite my mad dash from one wing of the airport to another, I missed my connection to the commuter flight to Monterey.

I decided to make the almost three-hour drive from San Francisco down to Monterey in a rental car, starting at about 11:30 p.m. I know I can fall asleep while driving pretty easily, so I found myself a huge cup of coffee and started singing loud and long as soon as I got in the car. I sang just about every hymn and praise song I could remember. Then I prayed aloud. Then I sang some more. For some reason the hymn "Great Is Thy Faithfulness" kept coming to mind, and I probably sang it thirty times that night.

After I had been driving for almost two hours, I turned off Highway 101 onto the connecting highway and, just to make it a "perfect" trip, I hit road construction ... at 1:30 a.m. I had the opportunity to park and watch paving trucks go to and fro for fifteen minutes. I started asking God rather firmly what else he was trying to teach me that very long evening. While I often respond to these kinds of situations with frustration, that particular evening became one of the best prayer and praise times I had had in some time. But the lesson is that in our busy schedules, we can take those unexpected events and use them to God's glory. Instead of becoming painful memories, they can be opportunities to draw closer to our heavenly Father. While I was physically tired the next morning, I was spiritually recharged like I hadn't been for weeks.

Finally, I encourage my family to do likewise. I regularly ask each of my children how they are doing and what they are reading in their devotion times. I ask them what they are learning through their personal time in the Word and if they have questions that I might help them to answer. I also tell them what I'm reading and learning.

I encourage them to ask me about my devotions as well. This idea of mutual accountability with your children can be powerful in your life as well as theirs.

Recently, I was pretty astonished when our second son, Nathan, approached me on one of his trips home from college. When we found some time to meet quietly and talk alone, I was startled that he confronted me over some areas regarding his younger brother, Micah. In particular, he felt I wasn't spending enough time with Micah due to my busy work schedule. Since Nathan was off at college, he knew he wasn't there to stay close to Micah, and he saw that I wasn't either. I was quite startled and appreciated the wake-up call. The idea of mutual accountability, even to and with your children, is a very powerful one. If you are willing to be open and vulnerable with your family, you might be quite astonished at the increased depth in relationship you will have.

CHURCH

One of the areas where we demonstrate our commitment to God is through the church and our active participation there. As Christ departed this earth, he left behind three primary institutions to guide all of humankind into a relationship with the Father: his Word (John 1:1), his Spirit (John 14:15–17), and his church (Matt. 16:18).

Throughout the mission trips of Paul and the other apostles recorded in the book of Acts, we see them establishing the local church as the structured place for the Christians to gather, proclaim the Word, and develop relationships for support and accountability:

Paul and Barnabas appointed elders for them in each church and, with prayer and fasting, committed them to the Lord, in whom they had put their trust. (Acts 14:23)

As we see in consistent references throughout the New Testament, the church became the basic unit of Christianity (Matt. 16:18; Acts 8:1-3; Acts 9:31; Acts 11:22).

Finally, we see an admonition by the writer of Hebrews that we should never give up meeting together with believers. The church was the place, the mechanism for God's people to constantly come together to encourage one another.

Let us not give up meeting together, as some are in the habit of doing, but let us encourage one another—and all the more as you see the Day approaching. (Heb. 10:25)

The practical question, however, is what should we do with respect to the church as busy individuals with far too many priorities on our respective plates? First, the Hebrews passage above establishes the requirement of all believers to participate regularly in a church. I find no basis for "Easter and Christmas only" Christians. I also find no basis for substituting individual worship "wherever you find God." The church is the gathering place for teaching, proclaiming the Word, publicly declaring God's praises, holding each other accountable, and worshipping as a community.

We must not simply slide into the back of the church around the end of the first hymn and slip out just prior to the altar call, either. The church was established as the command center for Christ's work on earth. The church is the place for teaching and instruction in the truth (Acts 2:42). It's the place for prayer needs of the body to be lifted up as a group before the Father (Acts 12:12). It's also the place for the gathering of finances to support needs of believers both locally and abroad (2 Cor. 8:19). It's the place where missionaries are set apart and sent out (Acts 13). It's the place where matters of doctrine are discussed (Acts 15:4–7). It's the location for new believers to make their public confessions (Acts 2:41).

Based on this and many other references throughout the New Testament, I see one's relationship with God being demonstrated through active participation in the local church. This could mean teaching and preaching, mission work, leadership, taking the offering and serving Communion, as a prayer warrior, support of the elderly, serving as a deacon or elder, maintenance of the church properties, and so on.

As I mentioned in chapter 1, I have served two terms for a total of eight years as an elder in our congregation. Early every Monday morning we would have an elder prayer time for the congregation where for an hour or two we lift up specifically each and every prayer request from that week's service. All of the elders would regularly call on those in our respective shepherding groups. As I've stepped back from this capacity right now, I feel I was uniquely called for the period of eldership I served. We had some difficult leadership transitions to manage through during this period. Also, while serving as elder, I heard God speaking specifically through me to handle some troubling, difficult leadership decisions on three specific occasions. I expect someday I'll again be in the position of eldership at our local congregation.

Throughout the years, Linda and I have had a Bible study in our home, which I led or co-led. By hosting these study times, we've developed some deep and lasting friendships that now span many states through the normal transition of jobs and locations. We've seen several friends progress in faith and several come to Christ through these home studies. We now have a different structure of small groups that rotates through different homes, and we happily host when it's our turn. I also periodically teach classes and occasionally preach on Sunday mornings.

If you are not in a study, consider it carefully. If you are in one, consider leading one. Of course, if you have a travel schedule like mine, you will probably need to carefully choose a co-leader who can fill in when you aren't there, or simply make yourself available when you are in town. Occasionally I've been traveling so much and miss a few consecutive weeks that I'll get a well-deserved introduction as a visitor or traveling lecturer upon my return!

On the other end of the spectrum, church tasks can become nothing but another set of overwhelming and endless activities. *Church* work can become no different than *work* work. We can so easily lose sight of our relationship with the Father as we zealously pursue our church jobs, just like the religious leaders of Jesus' day. This lack of focus brought a startling, strong rebuke from Christ:

> Everything they do is done for men to see: They make their phylacteries wide and the tassels on their garments long. (Matt. 23:5)

Our church work can literally consume all the time we have for God. As Martha did in her time with Jesus, we can lose sight of the Savior (Luke 10:38–42). Church activities cannot replace a relationship with Christ, but they can displace it.

As an elder at my church, for example, I was responsible for keeping in touch with and praying for about twenty-five families. Given my other demands, I found this overwhelming and ultimately impossible. My church service became a source of anxiety and guilt. Other elders felt the same. I'm happy to say we eventually found a solution that involved recruiting, training, and empowering some undershepherds. But that was a Martha-like case where, for a time, serving God became a burden that crushed all the joy and sense of accomplishment I might get from being an elder.

As will be a recurring theme throughout this book, we need proper priorities and then proper balance against those priorities. Putting God first is critical, and to put God first means you also include a solid commitment to an active local church life.

FINANCES

Throughout the Gospels, we see Jesus talking frequently about money. We see that how we handle finances is critically important to our Savior (Luke 16:14–15). He emphasizes how our finances can become a distraction or a replacement for our relationship with God (Matt. 6:24). He addresses the manner in which we acquire money (Luke 3:14). He teaches on indebtedness (Luke 7:42–43). How we give to the Lord's work is critically important as well (Mark 12:41–44). He addresses sensitive issues like taxation (Matt. 17:24–27). He also addresses how we use and invest our finances

(Mark 14:4–9; Matt. 25:14–30; Luke 19:11–27). One cannot finish a thoughtful reading of the Gospels and the remainder of the New Testament without realizing that to Christ and the church how we handle money is clearly a part of our relationship with the Father. If we are going to have God as our first priority, we will handle our finances in a manner consistent with biblical truths.

I would suggest a few principles that can guide our handling of finances. We'll cover the first three of these here and the fourth in chapter 4.

Moving from:

1. Tithe to Sacrifice
2. Debt to Inheritance
3. Giving to Blessing
4. Controversy to Agreement

FROM TITHE TO SACRIFICE

I've always appreciated the life and preaching of John Wesley, the great English evangelist who both authored and subsequently delivered countless sermons as he rode from town to town. His saddle, equipped with a bookshelf so he could study while he rode, remains evidence of his dedication. He made three interesting, if not surprising, points on finances: *Make all you can, save all you can,* and *give all you can.*

Make all you can. Work hard and seek to be a successful, great employee who is rewarded suitably (see chapter 5). We shouldn't be ashamed to receive God's blessing into our lives.

Save all you can. Be frugal. Carefully plan your finances and budget (Luke 14:28); do a great job with your investments, gifts, and talents (Matt. 25:14–30). Linda and I began developing a budget from the outset of our marriage. At the time, we really needed one as the dollars were pretty thin and the demands of a growing family in the expensive California Bay Area were significant. Over the years, we've moved from budgeting in order to make ends meet to carefully planning our investments and developing an inheritance for our children and grandchildren. I believe that some of our current financial blessings are a direct result of the financial habits and tithing that began when we could barely make ends meet.

Finally, **give all you can.** One purpose of both earning and saving is to be able to give generously to the Lord's work. It is discouraging to see statistics showing that believers of all faiths give only a marginally higher percentage of their income to charities than do those who claim no association with any faith (2.5 percent versus 2.2 percent). Furthermore, those from wealthy, industrialized nations are only modestly more charitable than those from developing countries. This level of giving is so low it's startling.

If we use the Old Testament tithe of 10 percent as a starting point for giving, we fall far short. Moreover, we see the New Testament taking the Old Testament guidelines and turning them into more powerful principles for Christian living (1 Tim. 6:18, Acts 2:42–47, and 2 Cor. 9:11). Thus, it would be appropriate that we as Christians would be giving more under the new covenant than the old. Instead, however, our freedom from the Old Testament law appears to have become an excuse for selfishness and materialism.

You will be made rich in every way so that you can be generous
on every occasion, and through us your generosity will result in
thanksgiving to God. (2 Cor. 9:11)

The verse quoted above can be taken to apply to both physical
riches and spiritual matters. The same Greek root word is used
clearly for financial matters as well as spiritual matters in the New
Testament. From this I'd suggest a principle that results from holding
God as our first priority: Give an increasing percentage of all we
make to charity and the work of the Lord.

As we mature in the faith and increase our financial well-being
over the course of our lives and career, we need to become increasingly
focused on applying our wealth to his kingdom and purposes. Apply
this principle and amazing things can begin to occur. Imagine how
God can bless you if you are consistently pouring your finances back
into his work.

Maybe you're not used to giving regularly, however. You might
even be struggling to make ends meet. Giving 10 percent of your
income back to God may seem just impossible in your current
financial situation. In such a case, let me suggest you start giving just
1 or 2 percent and see what happens. Make that the first check you
write each month. I believe you'll find God faithful to reward that
step of faith by supplying all of your needs.

From there, as God prospers you, you can add another
percentage point to your giving each year. When you do that, as
Linda and I have, you'll see God's blessings in your life in ever-
increasing ways. Eventually, you can be giving 20 percent, 30
percent, and even more to his work. Our family goal is to get to

where we're giving more than half of our yearly gross income to the Lord and his work.

As you can see from my personal mission statement in chapter 2, Linda and I aim to increase our giving every year. Look specifically at goal 8: *Give an increasing portion of all I earn to charity: church, missions, and other Christian organizations.* This is meant mathematically as it is written: Every year we give an increasing percentage of our total gross income to charities. While your mission statement is an entirely personal matter, I'd sure like yours to include something similar to this item. It would be great to give God the opportunity to bless your life with the overflowing abundance that comes from a giver's heart.

The father of our former home church's minister was the man who first taught me this idea of giving an increasing percentage of income. The father was a successful physician and had lived a nicely successful career. He and his wife had gotten to the point where they were giving 80 percent of their total income to the Lord's work. I was blown away when I heard him describe this principle and how he had lived it.

However, giving our money is only the beginning of sacrificial giving to God's work. Before we give to a ministry, we need to carefully investigate the ministry and be convinced it is true to its mission and purpose, follows careful financial accountability, and is aligned with our objectives. One of Linda's spiritual gifts is being a giver. However, she is very cautious and skeptical about her giving until a ministry is proven and validated. Once it is, and if she has a passion for it, she's ready to give the bank account—all of it!

Further, we need to be actively involved in the ministries we support. Linda and I thoroughly discuss, prayerfully consider, and carefully study charities before we give to them. We understand the mission and work of the institution and also have developed a level of personal relationship with the individuals involved.

We support several missionaries in Kenya, for example. During an earlier sabbatical and vacation, we visited them for several weeks. This was a great time of visiting our friends but also an opportunity to participate in the work firsthand. Last summer Linda and Micah spent several weeks in Kenya working in an orphanage and slum area with our missionary friends. When we talk to others about these ministries, we can speak with firsthand knowledge about their work.

We also need to follow our giving with our thoughts and prayers. Do you stay actively involved with the ministries you support? Are you certain your finances are being used in the manner you expect? Do you know the current needs of the ministry? Do you continue to uphold these charities and ministries in regular prayer?

DEBT TO INHERITANCE

The top 15 percent of the world's population consumes 75 percent of all goods and services the world produces. A stunning one-third of the world's population lives on less than $1,000 per year.[3] Despite the enormous wealth of the United States and other developed countries, being the most prosperous isn't sufficient; we are also the greatest debtors on earth. The insatiable hunger of materialism forever cries for more, demanding we seek greater and greater indebtedness.

The Bible speaks clearly regarding debt—don't do it. Debt was harshly discouraged under Mosaic law, as interest or any form of indebtedness to other Israelites was forbidden (Prov. 28:8; Ezek. 18:8, 13, 17; 22:12; Ps. 15:5). All debts were to be cancelled in the year of Jubilee (Deut. 15:1–11). We see that the debtor became enslaved in one manner or another to the debt holder, leading to long-term moral or spiritual decay.

> If you lack the means to pay, your very bed will be snatched from under you. (Prov. 22:27)

> Do not charge your brother interest, whether on money or food or anything else that may earn interest. You may charge a foreigner interest, but not a brother Israelite, so that the LORD your God may bless you in everything you put your hand to in the land you are entering to possess. (Deut. 23:19–20)

In contrast, Scripture encourages a lifestyle marked by freedom from all manner of debt, minimizing our concern for financial needs and preparing an inheritance for the generations to come.

> For where your treasure is, there your heart will be also. (Matt. 6:21)

> Wisdom, like an inheritance, is a good thing and benefits those who see the sun. (Eccl. 7:11)

> A good man leaves an inheritance for his children's children, but a sinner's wealth is stored up for the righteous. (Prov. 13:22)

While this may sound easy, we know that it's difficult to live consistently in this manner. If you are under a burden of debt, change your lifestyle to conserve, and build a plan to begin the slow, hard process of working your way out of debt. If credit cards give you difficulty, cut them up and discard them before they lead you further into misery. If you have difficulty sticking to your budget, establish a system where each month you first take out all the money required for household expenses—food, savings, charities, and so on. Apply them to the budget items before using any funds for discretionary spending. I'd also suggest you study and apply some of the many fine Christian materials written on finances, such as those by Ron Blue.

I have a close friend who has seen the need to simplify his financial state and get to the point where his wife no longer needs to work outside the home. They are shedding possessions, selling rental homes and other possessions, and putting themselves on a path that will steadily move them closer to freedom from debt. Another friend, realizing he couldn't give a consistent offering to the Lord's work, is planning to decrease the size of his mortgage by moving to a smaller home. I applaud the efforts of both men. They are making and carrying out tough decisions to move from debt to inheritance. While these are tough decisions for them to make, and their families are making sacrifices for them, I am seeing the freedom and confidence it is bringing to both men and their families.

Some financial writers suggest that having a mortgage is fine, if not recommended. Not only do you garner a physical asset—the home—but you also get the benefit of favorable tax handling of mortgage interest. Certainly, a mortgage is often superior financially to paying rent, which offers no long-term financial reward. And, for almost everyone, a mortgage is the only possible way to ever own a home.

Some continue even further and argue that a mortgage is a great investment due to the tax write-off you receive. While you can run the numbers for your own situation, you'll probably find that you come out an interest point or two ahead if you use a mortgage as an investment compared to most other low-risk investments. However, I believe strongly that the biblical principle of "no debt" should take precedence over the potential for a mere point or two of financial gain in elongating or even increasing your mortgage.

Thus, while a mortgage is a clear requirement for most, I'd challenge you to get out of debt, all of it, including your mortgage, as quickly as your financial situation allows. Of course, for a mortgage this could take quite a number of years. Get started anyway. In most compounding interest-rate loans, even modest increases in your monthly payment will take years off the life of the loan. While paying a bit more each month on an already stretched budget may not sound too exciting, you will begin to whittle away years of that mortgage rather quickly. Increasing your monthly payment just 10 percent could take 7 years or 23 percent off the duration of a 30-year mortgage. Increasing your payments just 15 percent could take almost 10 years or 30 percent off the duration of a 30-year mortgage.

While today Linda and are I financially very well off, we began our thrust to debt-free living at the start of our marriage when a tight budget was a necessity. A technician's wage at Intel wasn't much when you factor in California's cost of living! Linda and I started paying extra on our 30-year mortgage just a couple of years after our marriage and our first mortgage began. We increased our payments by 10 percent, then 15 percent, and 25 percent as our financial blessings allowed. We then refinanced our remaining mortgage when interest rates allowed us to move to a 15-year loan for a better interest rate. After moving to a new location, we again took out a 15-year loan. We were excited about the thought of being entirely out of debt, and we immediately began paying off our new mortgage more rapidly as well.

Also, speaking momentarily only to men, imagine a conversation with your wife sometime in the future that might go something like this: "Dear, we have absolutely no debt. The house is paid for, and we have saved up finances sufficient for us to live a modest but comfortable life should either of us be unable to provide any longer for our household. We've left a biblical inheritance for our children and their children as well."

Wow, what a powerful statement! Imagine the anniversary celebration where you could burn your mortgage papers, celebrating the end of your indebtedness. While for most this will be a long, slow process, such a commitment will yield incredible fruits in this life and in the one to come.

GIVING TO BLESSING

Most of us, particularly men, are excited about the potential for a prize or reward. Maybe it's a track event where we're focused on winning the medal or trophy. Maybe in fishing we're out to catch the trophy fish. Maybe we're working to take a few strokes off our golf score and be the best in our foursome. Maybe in our work we're eager to win an award, earn a promotion, or receive a raise. God made us such that we look forward to prizes or gifts. We shouldn't be ashamed to say we are eager for the prize or the rewards we are promised.

Personally, I'm very goal oriented. I'm out to win the prize. I'm eagerly looking forward to the blessings that God promised for a lifestyle of consistent and faithful giving to his work.

> Remember this: Whoever sows sparingly will also reap sparingly, and whoever sows generously will also reap generously.... Now he who supplies seed to the sower and bread for food will also supply and increase your store of seed and will enlarge the harvest of your righteousness. You will be made rich in every way so that you can be generous on every occasion, and through us your generosity will result in thanksgiving to God. (2 Cor. 9:6, 10–11)

> Give, and it will be given to you. A good measure, pressed down, shaken together and running over, will be poured into your lap. For with the measure you use, it will be measured to you. (Luke 6:38)

Some read these passages and conclude that they offer an entirely spiritual benefit. I heartily agree that you will be blessed spiritually by a life of consistent and increasing giving to God's work. I receive a blessing every time the missionaries we support report progress in their ministry, and when they count the new believers, I rejoice joining with the legions of angels. I receive a blessing every time the church-planting organization we support launches a new congregation. Every time a new member joins our church or a new person is baptized into Christ, I take a personal blessing from the occasion.

However, from reading the context of those passages and from the Greek words used, there is no basis for a strictly spiritual interpretation. I've heard and read countless stories of people giving in faith, only to be rewarded with near immediate "surprises" from God's generosity meeting their physical needs. You receive blessings now and in the future, both spiritual and physical, for a life of faithful stewardship.

Also, God understands how finances work, and if the inflow is decreasing, the outflow can't continue to increase. Some have taken from these verses what is called the law of the harvest:[4]

- You reap after you sow.
- You reap what you sow.
- You reap more than you sow.

First comes your confidence in God to provide for your needs as you give. You cannot expect a blessing in response to greed or a love for money (1 Tim. 6:9–10; Titus 3:14). Blessings come as a result of our love for the Father and our generosity for his kingdom and its work on earth.

Second, you reap of the kind you sow. Did you sow abundantly or sparingly? Did you sow with a spirit of generosity and sacrifice as we see with the widow in Mark 12:42–44?

Finally, you receive more than you sow. Your investments into kingdom work will be rewarded with blessings that continue to multiply. It truly is more blessed to give than to receive (Acts 20:35). As God challenges us through the prophet Malachi:

"Bring the whole tithe into the storehouse, that there may be food in my house. Test me in this," says the LORD Almighty, "and see if I will not throw open the floodgates of heaven and pour out so much blessing that you will not have room enough for it." (Mal. 3:10)

· · · · ·

In summary, we've covered three of four principles on godly finances, with the fourth to come in chapter 4:

1. Tithe to Sacrifice: Give an increasing percentage of all you have to charity.
2. Debt to Inheritance: Commit today to cease from all kinds of debt and pursue an inheritance for your children and grandchildren.
3. Giving to Blessing: Look forward to the rewards of a life of godly stewardship.
4. Controversy to Agreement (to be covered in chapter 4).

We need to place God as our first priority in order to live a balanced life and succeed in our juggling act. This will be seen in our daily time with him. We will, as we've done on several topics in this chapter, apply the truth of his Word directly into our daily lives. We'll be regular and active in his body, the church. Finally, we will place the critical matter of our finances in submission to him.

· · · · ·

CHAPTER 3 QUESTIONS

1. How can you make and keep God your number one priority in life?

2. Do you find your religious regimen ever getting to the point where it is little more than a daily routine? How can you put more of yourself into your personal devotions and prayer?

3. Is it wise for someone who travels heavily or puts in late nights at work to commit to leading a weekly Bible study? How can you fit your home Bible study into an already taxing schedule?

4. How can you make your finances reflect God as the highest priority in your life?

5. How do you deal with work assigned to you on a Sunday?

4

. . . . .

Prioritizing Family Time

. . . . .

LEE AND ANNE MARIE, close friends of our family and members of our church, decided they had been led by God to take their family to the mission field. After over a year of preparation, they left in January 1998 to begin their first mission experience. Anxious to visit and encourage our friends, we made the long trip that summer with our oldest children, Elizabeth and Josiah, to visit them in Kenya. We decided that Micah and Nathan weren't quite old enough at that time to make the trip. Shortly after our return, Micah was in his room one night having his personal devotion time. Linda was pretty strict when our kids were young that when they were in bed, they were in bed, and unless it was an emergency, that is where they were to stay. Thus, when Micah came out of his room that night, Linda was quick to begin correcting him and ready to firmly send him back to bed. When our young eight-year-old announced with bold confidence, "God wants me to be a missionary to Kenya," we were both blown away but also skeptical. Linda and I figured that was like a kid saying, "I want to be a firefighter," or, "I want to be president," or, "I'll be a pro basketball player," and that he'd quickly grow out of it. So, we smiled in affirmation and kept our doubts to ourselves. However, in 2001, on my third every-seven-year sabbatical from Intel, we made a trip as a family—with Micah this time—that included three weeks in Kenya. We visited Lee and Anne Marie, as well as missionary friends Keith and Kathy who were working with the Turkana people in the desolate, drought-stricken northern part of the country, just below the Sahara.

At the end of that time, Micah said, "Thanks, Mom and Dad, for bringing us here. I really appreciate it. And I still want to be a missionary to Kenya!"

That experience demonstrates the value of two things: making time to help your children develop a heart for God, and making time for family vacations. As you'll see in this chapter, I haven't always done a good job with such things.

Deuteronomy 6:5–9 says,

> Love the LORD your God with all your heart and with all your soul and with all your strength. These commandments that I give you today are to be upon your hearts. Impress them on your children. Talk about them when you sit at home and when you walk along the road, when you lie down and when you get up. Tie them as symbols on your hands and bind them on your foreheads. Write them on the doorframes of your houses and on your gates.

As I've read and studied this passage of Scripture over the years, I've grown in both excitement and passion for it. Read it again and let the words of Moses fill not only your mind but also your heart.

Let your eyes well with tears as you see how passionate God is for his Word—how he desires that it be affirmed by parents and embedded into the lives of their children.

Over many generations, this passage led to the development of the phylactery, which is handed down by Orthodox Jews to this day as the outward symbol of the Word of God in their lives. They literally bind pouches holding Scriptures to their hands and foreheads as visible and physical evidence of their love for God's Word. Oh, the love and passion for God's Word the author intended for us to possess. How vital he realized it was for this passion to be handed from parents to their children. Can you read Psalm 119 and not be urged to be ever more passionate for God's Word, "Thy word is a lamp unto my feet!" (v. 105 KJV)?

While most of you reading this are probably not of Jewish descent, I'd challenge you to consider this passage with the same passion as Moses intended. What are your family beliefs and practices, and how will you pass them to the next generation? What are your morals and ethical standards, and how will your family learn to hold these true and critical for their life's work?

In our interconnected, real-time-communicating world we are bombarded with a diverse set of choices: People can choose from an almost infinite pool of lifestyles and religious and philosophic frameworks. As our children are confronted with this dizzying array, our job is not to simply offer up a full à la carte menu of the alternatives. No, we parents need to develop in our children a solid framework and understanding of our beliefs and traditions, working with them to develop their own personal beliefs that will govern them for the remainder of their lives. Further, we need to model for them those values and convictions in the best classroom of all—our daily lives.

In this chapter we'll explore some tools to help you find time to make that kind of impact in your children's lives.

BREAKFAST ONE-ON-ONE

Almost twenty years ago, when our daughter, Elizabeth, was just five years old, I started a practice of taking her out for breakfast once each month. As the boys came along, I then had two, then three, and finally four kids to take to monthly breakfast. I would have breakfast with one of the kids every week on a rotating basis. It used to be even a cheap way to have some special one-on-one time with each of them. We would usually share a breakfast, which they would choose and which made it even more enjoyable. As the kids have gotten older, however, they refuse to share their food with me anymore. Instead they demand their own breakfast and, particularly the boys, usually consume part of mine as well.

Over the years, the kids grew to look forward to these times: a special one-on-one time with Dad. When I returned home with the designated child of the morning, the siblings would always say, "Where did you go?" and, "What did you have to eat?" … "You're lucky it was your turn." Sometimes, I'd drop the child off at school after breakfast on my way to work, which made it even more special.

Of course, with a busy travel schedule, I didn't make breakfasts happen each week. But I asked my administrative assistant to both schedule and prioritize my breakfast meetings with the kids.

Sometimes it took a bit of calendar gymnastics, but usually, we were able to get them scheduled in. When I started doing this, I had a simple thought in mind: Maybe if I start with them while they're young, it will become enough of a habit that when they hit those rough teenage years, we will have at least some venue for continued conversation.

The breakfast agenda is pretty simple. I require from the child a formal, written agenda with minutes from our last breakfast, updates on the action items agreed upon at our last meeting, and a new and proposed specific list of topics for this one.

Just kidding. I have no agenda whatsoever. The real agenda is whatever the kids want to talk about. I usually try to have at least one topic in mind to get to somewhere in the course of the conversation. This might be an issue at home, something that's on my heart about them, a Scripture, or a spiritual topic. We'd always discuss how school is going, how they are doing spiritually, and anything that is troubling them.

As the kids have gotten older, they have started to store up questions or issues that they want to discuss. Sometimes it's stuff related to homework. Sometimes we'd have papers and books spread across the table at the restaurant. Other times, they want to discuss items related to their spiritual life. On one occasion, my daughter had three or four Scripture passages she was having trouble understanding. I felt like I was on a Bible-trivia show; they were tough passages. I am so proud to see them looking forward to this time and planning how they can take advantage of it.

After doing this for many years, it was rare that a child didn't want to take his or her turn. Occasionally, one would give an "I'm too tired." If so, I would just go to the next kid in the rotation; and with four to choose from, it was unusual if I couldn't coax at least one of the kids into breakfast with good old Dad.

With three of the kids now out of the house, the breakfast rotation is now pretty ad hoc. But, whenever they are in town or available, we still try to get out for a similar one-on-one time. Often this is at a local Starbucks or such. In fact, during a recent busy time, Elizabeth wanted to do breakfast with me. I was astonished when she agreed to meet me at 5:00 a.m. before I headed off to the airport. You couldn't imagine a prouder dad than I was that day.

I also tried every weekend to spend time one-on-one with each kid when they were still living at home. This might have been them sitting on my lap while we read a book when they were little, playing basketball, playing a board game, playing cards, helping with homework, working out at the gym together, doing some chores together, playing racquetball or tennis, going to the driving range, playing nine or eighteen holes, or just sitting and talking about school or sports. On Sunday afternoon or evening, before the weekend was over and another frantic week began, I did a quick mental checklist and asked myself, *Have I spent time with each of them? Have I had a chance just to connect with all of them individually?* If not, I'd quickly try to correct my oversight and ask what they'd like to do.

Similarly, I'm trying to talk to them at least each week when they are off at college or on their own. It's far too easy to lose track of them when I don't see them in the house on a regular basis.

A close friend recently told me that he does "alone time" with his kids. Each weekend he has an activity that he does with each one of his kids individually. I had another dad tell me that after he heard my method from me, he started doing breakfasts with each of his kids and, like our family, it's become a rich time for them.

Through these times with my kids, my goal is to learn to know them deeply. What are their unique character qualities? What do they like and enjoy? What are their areas of weakness for which I need to be praying? How are they uniquely gifted by God? As the Proverb indicates,

> Train a child in the way he should go, and when he is old he will not turn from it. (Prov. 22:6)

Note, this says "in the way he should go," not the way you've decided he should go. Darby's translation gives a bit more insight: "according to the tenor of his way." This indicates a certain bent or natural inclination unique to each child. Maybe you love football and your son loves music. Should you force him into your tenor and require him to play football, or learn to appreciate and encourage his enjoyment for music and look forward to his concerts and recitals? Should your career or family business become his, or should you learn his bent to help him choose a profession that uniquely matches his God-given gifts and talents? This is most difficult for us fathers to do. Right now it looks like none of my kids will end up in engineering or technology, and this was a bit challenging for me to accept. I'm an engineer and love it. Shouldn't my kids want to be one too?

Before heading off to begin his freshman year at college, Nathan came to me, asking to talk. He was very concerned. As we've noted already, Nathan is studying music and youth ministry, and desires a position in full-time ministry. He feared that I wouldn't approve of his career choice. He was concerned that he was choosing a profession that wouldn't be very lucrative, as mine had been. He feared that by not choosing to follow in my footsteps, he wouldn't be successful in my eyes. I was astonished. I couldn't imagine that I'd been anything but strongly supportive of his choice of profession to this point. However, there he was with tears in his eyes, crying out for my approval. He was simply seeking my blessing. He wanted to be certain that I—his father—approved of the path he was choosing.

I responded to him that of course I did. When we arrive in heaven, the only currency that matters is how many lives we are able to touch for the kingdom of Christ. Wealth and fame are fleeting, but touching lives for Christ is an eternal result. In fact, Nathan, with his talents and gifting, will probably be more successful than I am. He will touch more for eternity than I will. Indeed, I am confident he will have greater success than I on the scales of eternity.

I've enjoyed trying to guess what sports or musical instrument each of our children might like based on his or her character qualities. I've also enjoyed trying to guess their potential professions based on their giftedness. I've prayed specifically for insights into how to raise and encourage them.

I recall recently a family camp weekend where Michael Smalley was the speaker. As a Christian psychologist, he had us take a personality test, and he subsequently encouraged us to have our children do likewise. I thought I had studied our children pretty well, but while I could predict the results accurately for three of our kids, I couldn't tell where Josiah would show up. When I saw his results, I went, "Wow!" All of a sudden I saw how his naturally quiet personality was hiding some strong leadership characteristics. This also explained several areas where I was struggling with him and didn't understand why we were having these conflicts. It was exciting to realize the source of the conflict and suddenly have new insights into how to improve our relationship.

FAMILY VACATIONS

As I've already admitted, I tend to work long and hard. It should come as no surprise that in the past I have viewed taking vacations as entirely discretionary. In the first ten years of my career at Intel, I averaged less than one week a year of vacation. Being so busy with school, I almost always found myself with more than I could hope to accomplish at work. Besides, I loved what I was doing at work and school. So why would I stop and go off to do something boring like rest and relax? I was loving work, so ... do more of it!

Then one day my lovely and patient wife, Linda, sat me down and gave me a totally different perspective: While *I* may not need those things called vacation times, the family needed me on vacation. It was imperative that we spend that time together and build those memories that we will share for years to come. It sounds so simple, but amazingly I didn't get it until she challenged me in this way.

Of course, she was right. As Linda will resoundingly affirm, it's not often that I'll immediately admit that she's right and I'm simply and entirely wrong. This time, without hesitation, I had to say, "Yes, you're right. Forgive me." Since that talk, our family has not missed a single day of vacation to which I am entitled.

We try to make a big deal out of our vacations. We plan and talk about them considerably as a family. We take big trips and small. In fact, I wrote a good amount of this book's first edition while taking my third sabbatical from Intel. We traveled through Europe, including London, Paris, Switzerland, Germany, and Austria, and then spent three weeks in Kenya.

We had a wonderful time seeing these many countries, cities, and cultures as well as visiting several missionary friends in Kenya and going on several safaris. We followed this with family time at our vacation home and a camping trip. We did a trip to Disney World, the Caicos Islands in the Caribbean, and some time at a family reunion on the East Coast. The kids consider this one of our best vacations ever.

Other years we've traveled to national parks or to the East Coast for time with my parents. On other occasions, Linda and I have had romantic trips for just the two of us to Thailand, Australia, and Hawaii. We did a big family trip to New Zealand and Australia. We also did a family trip to Banff and Jasper, Canada, one year.

We've also tried to carve more vacation time out of our normal routines. We will spend a long weekend or school break skiing or at the beach. We purchased a vacation home as a place to develop more of those family memories. It gives us even more opportunities to get away as a family or with a few of the kids' friends. As soon as the school calendar comes out, I'll have my assistant start marking three- and four-day weekends off on my calendar. Sometimes I need to work on those days from our vacation home, but we still get substantially more family time in as a result of just being away.

While family time is always at a premium, you'll be amazed at how much togetherness you can squeeze in with a little planning.

Add a strong effort to protect those special times, and you'll start to build tremendous family memories.

If you haven't yet gotten into the habit of making family vacations a priority, I'd recommend you begin doing so.

DATE YOUR SPOUSE

I'm pleasantly surprised when I talk to people who regularly date their spouses. I'm also astonished at the number of people I talk to who can't remember the last time they had a date with their spouse. Too many times, couples have allowed their entire focus to shift to their children. They invest all their finances, all their time, and all their emotional energy in their children. Of course, children need huge quantities of all three. However, we must give our marriages even higher priority than our relationships with our children.

Only from a strong marriage comes a strong family. A strong marriage establishes a foundation for your home in which to raise your children. The most recent census data, unfortunately, showed a continuing decline in households with both the mother and father of the children present—now less than 25 percent of all homes in the United States. Obviously, far too many people have failed to prioritize the relationships with their spouses.

The marriage bond must be held as our most important human relationship. In Genesis we see this powerful command:

> For this reason a man will leave his father and mother and be united
> to his wife, and they will become one flesh. (Gen. 2:24)

I like to choose slightly different words for each of the three commands we see there. They create a nice rhythmic trio that makes the commands more memorable:

1. *A man shall leave his father and mother.* This is the point in his life when he severs the cords of dependency he has had with his parents.

2. *He is to cleave to his wife.* He should exchange the dependent relationship with his parents for an interdependent relationship with his wife.

3. *Finally, they shall weave their lives together, becoming one flesh.* They are to meld their lives into a single entity, intertwining their values, activities, and goals.[5]

I suggest you and your spouse consider this model carefully: Leave, cleave, and weave. Lacking this focus on the marriage bond leaves the entire family structure on shifting sand. Soon those children will begin to leave the nest and, all of a sudden, you will be living with a stranger. You will have lost any semblance of an intimate relationship with this one called your spouse.

At one point many years ago, Linda was becoming extremely busy with the children. This wasn't too surprising, considering we had four children combined with my hectic travel schedule. In fact, this was almost to be expected. Feeling uneasy about a few instances where it felt as if she had prioritized the kids above everything else, including me, I questioned her one evening: "Linda, am I more important to you than the kids?" It was a difficult but important conversation, as both of us realized that we were letting our precious children squeeze between us.

We decided then and there that we couldn't allow that to occur, and we began making some priority choices. We made it a point to hug and kiss in front of the kids and not let them come between us when we did. We stopped letting them interrupt our conversations, even though young children always think their immediate wants are earth-shattering crises. We also were determined to stop sacrificing our times together.

Linda and I regularly date. While our dates are often spontaneous, we usually have at least one every month. Our goal is to date twice per month. When the kids were younger, dating required a lot of planning; now that they're older, it's much easier to be spontaneous.

Some of our dates are expensive, like dinner in a nice restaurant. But often we just grab a burger and go to a movie. Or we rent a video and pop our own popcorn at home. We may just go to Starbucks to talk for a while. Sometimes it's a walk around the neighborhood to get fresh air and work off the stresses of the day.

Linda and I also spend at least one weekend away each year. We call this our anniversary weekend and go to a beach house or hotel. Something like this can be so valuable for your marriage. Make these times special for you and your spouse, something that you can look forward to for weeks and then recall fondly for years afterward.

For instance, one year I started building up the excitement weeks in advance. You might have seen that little heart-shaped confetti you can buy at some drug stores. Each week for three weeks in advance, I'd hide those everywhere you could imagine—in her Bible, in her checkbook, in her shoes, in her pockets, in her makeup, in her car, on her pillow, in her jacket, and in her clothes drawer. Multiple times a day, she'd find them falling out from all over. She even became tired of picking them up.

For our actual weekend, I planned the location, bought her roses the color of our wedding roses, and had a bottle of sparkling cider waiting in the room. I also waxed poetic with one of the love notes we men hate to write. I gave her a new video camera to record more of our family times. I was excited to make this a special weekend and convey how important she is to me.

This past year we celebrated twenty-five years of wedded bliss together. It's hard to believe that anyone could live with me for that long. We planned a big vacation. We'd go to Athens for a few days and then on a Greek isle cruise and finally spend several days in Istanbul. On our actual anniversary day, which preceded our anniversary trip by several weeks, I gave her a card that said on the trip she had to make five purchases: something shiny, something that sparkles, something to keep her warm, something fun, and finally, something to remember our trip by. This just reinforced the anticipation Linda already had for our time away. The trip was wonderful, so much fun that we might not wait twenty-five more years to do another one like it!

Husbands, I challenge you, too, to just do it! Make the plans, hire the sitter, and create a special time for your wife. I'm sure you can be creative and plan special times uniquely suited to your spouse's tastes. Of course, wives, you can't overestimate the pleasure your husband receives when you take the initiative to plan a special evening for him, even if he's reluctant to admit it.

One time several years ago, I was traveling for a week in Europe, immediately followed by a week in Japan and Asia. In between I had a free weekend where I told Linda I would come home and spend time with her and the family. She thought I was nuts. She kept challenging me that instead of flying all the way home from Europe and then flying all the way to Japan, I should just go straight from Europe to Japan and spend a day or two getting some rest. Instead, through e-mail with several of her girlfriends, I planned a surprise birthday party for her on that weekend.

I landed on Saturday morning, and she and the kids picked me up at the airport. We spent some time as a family that afternoon. That evening, I had one of Linda's girlfriends come over to watch the kids, and we went to a hotel honeymoon suite downtown, where roses were waiting for her. The next morning we went to church, followed by dinner at a restaurant. When we arrived at the restaurant—surprise! Twenty-five of her friends were waiting to wish her a happy birthday. After the festivities, we went home, I packed for Japan and Asia, and zipped off to the airport. While it was only thirty hours at home, they were hours in which Linda felt extremely special.

FROM CONTROVERSY TO AGREEMENT

In chapter 3, we discussed the need to put our finances under God's leadership and manage them by his principles. We discussed three principles there, with a promise to cover a fourth in this chapter. Now that we've looked at the husband-wife relationship, we're ready to consider the idea of moving from Controversy to Agreement.

Over the years, I've seen a variety of surveys and writings on the causes for divorce. In almost all of them, finances are in the top three reasons. To resolve those problems, I'd like to suggest a simple but profound cure: "Just agree." Consider these words in the biblical book of Ephesians:

> Wives, submit to your husbands as to the Lord.… Now as the church submits to Christ, so also wives should submit to their husbands in everything. Husbands, love your wives, just as Christ loved the church and gave himself up for her.… In this same way, husbands ought to love their wives as their own bodies. He who loves his wife loves himself. (Eph. 5:22, 24–25, 28)

The principle taught in this passage is powerful—mutual submission. Now applying this idea to finances and marriage, instead of demanding your own way, you and your spouse each need to fully agree on every aspect of your family finances.

Make every major purchase a thoughtful, purposeful, and prayerful consideration between the two of you. Come into full agreement on all aspects of the purchase—cost, make, model, timing, and so on—before buying. If you don't agree, don't make the purchase until you do.

Some close friends told us the story of their recently married daughter and her young husband. The daughter decided she needed a new car. On her own, she went out and bought one that was far more expensive than they could afford. When her husband came home, she—with gleeful naïveté—announced the purchase as if he should appreciate her initiative and self-confidence. Well, the son-in-law's vehicle wasn't in particularly good condition. Justifying his opportunity, he went out and bought an even fancier model for himself the next day. As you might have expected, one new car payment was probably outside their budget and two new car payments were quick to break the bank. This is exactly the opposite of what I'm suggesting for mutual submission of finances.

We men often have greater difficulty with mutual financial submission than women do from two perspectives. First, we probably feel our role as head of the household gives us authority without accountability or submission to our wives. Second, as the old adage says, "The difference between men and boys is the price of their toys." Maybe we really don't need that new hunting rifle, sports car, golf clubs, boat, Jet Ski, ultralight fly rod, or off-road vehicle. While women might be more prone to an impromptu new outfit while shopping with some lady friends, they could buy ten or even a hundred new outfits for the price of some of our toys.

I recall a number of years ago when we had an encyclopedia salesman come to our house. I love books and the pursuit of knowledge. Not only did I want to get a set of encyclopedias, which I justified as "a great investment for the kids," but I also wanted to buy the entire set of "Great Books"—many of the classic writings of the last two millennia. Well, when the salesman came at the prearranged time, Linda had fallen ill and was lying in bed. Applying the "agree to agree on finances" principle, I kept shuttling from the living room with the salesman into the bedroom where sick Linda lay to discuss the potential purchase with her. After several treks back and forth, she finally succumbed to my desires. I was thrilled and eager for the arrival of my new books.

What a lousy purchase! No two ways about it; I had strong-armed Linda into agreeing with me. This single purchase has haunted me over the years as I realized I pressured her into it, particularly at a time when she wasn't feeling well. To this day we keep the "Great Books" prominently displayed, almost none of which have ever been opened, much less read. They serve as a constant reminder to me of the need for us to agree to agree. I doubt I'll ever put them away or sell them. I can use the constant reminder!

Apply this principle to all forms of investment as well. Invest nothing unless you and your spouse agree entirely. I find that we men are generally more willing to take higher risks, some of them foolishly or without due diligence. We'd put the house at risk for the promise of a great gain. Often our wives can provide a more balanced and cautious perspective.

When we first married, Linda viewed stocks and stock options as gambling and, thus, wrong. So we didn't do anything in the stock market. Occasionally, like when the big tech-bubble burst, her conservatism was well justified. In fact, holding firm to this principle, we almost allowed our first stock options to expire before exercising them. After a variety of explanations of how stocks are holdings with underlying assets of substance and value, we finally made it past the "this is gambling" conversation. We are now shareholders in a broad set of companies as one of our agreed-upon areas of investments. However, in some of the private start-up investments that we've done, we've not faired particularly well. While she agreed with me to make them, I should have been more sensitive to her reluctance and words of caution.

Apply these same principles to your discretionary and entertainment budgets. How much will you spend at work on lunches and the like, or should you take along a home-cooked meal and save a few dollars? How much should go toward monthly entertainment activities? How often will you eat out, and how much will you spend on restaurants? How much, if anything, will you give to the kids in allowances or in payment for chores? This simple topic of allowances is a great one for the two of you to work through. Before you are finished, you'll have set in place many of the principles for how you will teach your children the value of money. All of these should be discussed and agreed upon between you and your spouse.

Similarly, apply this to your charitable giving. Every place and amount should be decided in complete harmony between the two of you. Maybe you want to support a charity and your spouse isn't comfortable with it. Don't do it. Maybe you're convinced about the principle of continually increasing your financial giving as we discussed in chapter 3, but your spouse isn't. Don't do it.

Obviously, a conflict could arise between the principles of financial obedience to God and mutual submission to your spouse. How do you resolve it when you see two scriptural principles come into conflict? Which one do you choose to follow? While I don't see a clear or simple biblical resolution, I think submission to your spouse will provide a greater long-term gain. Tell your spouse of your desire to give to the charity and your belief that it's the appropriate way to honor God. However, out of submission to his or her desires, don't make the gift yet. Agree to agree with them before giving to this charity. After you've made this clear, prayerfully take this matter to God to change your heart or your spouse's. The change that results will help both of you to mature spiritually.

I counseled a Christian woman whose husband isn't yet a believer. The matter of giving had become a divisive issue between them. Instead of helping to draw him to Christianity, the issue was becoming another excuse for him to build a wall around his life. I advised her to submit to his wishes while still making clear her desires. We pray and hope that he might eventually be won over by his wife's behavior (1 Peter 3:1).

Applying this principle of mutual submission or "agree to agree" on all matters of finances can have powerful results in the husband-wife relationship. If you can't agree, don't do it. Choose a common amount and purpose for each aspect of your financial activities. After a year or two of doing this, your finances and your marriage should be in much better shape.

· · · · ·

In summary, the second major priority of our lives is family relationships. Prioritize your bond with your mate through dating and time away for the two of you. Manage your finances with mutual agreement. Build into your life regular times with your children. While juggling is never simple, with God and family clearly and properly prioritized, you'll be ready to consider the third major priority.

· · · · ·
CHAPTER 4 QUESTIONS

1. How can you prioritize your spouse above your children and profession?

2. Are regular dates with your spouse really necessary? Why?

3. How can you make family time a priority in your regular weekly activities?

4. How does your spouse manage alone with the kids when you're away?

5. How would you handle a spouse who is intensely busy, gone a lot, not involved in a church or the family, and not responsive to your suggestions to alter his or her priorities?

6. If your spouse is an extreme workaholic or simply refuses to adjust priorities, what can you do to improve the situation?

5

· · · · ·

Succeeding in
the Workplace

· · · · ·

AT INTEL, WE SOMETIMES have two people share a job for a time; we call them "two in a box" relationships. Sometimes it's because we've merged two groups, and this smoothens the transition. Other times, a job is just too big for one person. And still other times, it's a good way for a senior person to develop a younger one who might eventually take over the role entirely.

At one point fairly early in my career, I was paired in a box with a much more seasoned manager named Mike. I was aggressive and on a fast track; he was experienced and one of the best program managers I've ever seen anywhere.

On one occasion, we were both sent an e-mail asking for specific direction on a matter. I considered it to be a relatively minor topic. The message included a proposed course of action, and since the matter fell more on my side of the job responsibility, I shot back a quick "okay" without much thought.

Shortly thereafter, I got an e-mail from Mike. "It's not okay, and you know it," he said. "It's just not that important to you, and you aren't doing your job by letting it slide."

Wow, was I rebuked! And I deserved it. Mike was spot-on. I had been lazy and in a hurry to get the question out of my in-box. I learned a lesson that day that I've never forgotten: I'm going to handle everything I'm responsible for to the best of my ability, even when it's not my highest priority.

As outlined so far in this book: First, develop a plan for your life. Second, prioritize your personal relationship with God. And third, prioritize your family time. Now, that we've clearly laid out the scriptural priorities for your life, you should be ready to tackle the next priority: your profession or job.

I firmly believe that Christians should be the absolute best employees. We should be able to look at our work activities, and with confidence before our heavenly Father and earthly employer declare, "I've given the very best I have to offer." Christians should be the hardest working of them all. I'd emphasize, this is not an excuse for workaholism. However, in whatever hours we apply to our jobs—typically one-third or more of our waking hours—the message is simple: Do your best.

Scripture clearly and repeatedly supports this perspective.

Whatever you do, work at it with all your heart, as working for the Lord, not for men, since you know that you will receive an inheritance from the Lord as a reward. It is the Lord Christ you are serving. (Col. 3:23–24)

We see this theme communicated here and in Ephesians 4:28; 1 Thessalonians 4:11; 5:12–13; 2 Thessalonians 3:10; and 1 Corinthians 4:12; 9:6; 15:58. I'm not a theologian, but the simple rule of letting Scripture interpret Scripture is one of the basic tenets for any Bible student. In other words, if Scripture keeps repeating and elaborating on the same theme or topic, listen up.

Maybe I'm an idealist, but I'd like to believe that every Christian is a great employee. That's not because Christians are superior to non-Christians. Scripture clearly directs us to "in humility consider others better than [our]selves" (Phil. 2:3).

Instead, since we have—as Colossians tells us—an "inheritance from the Lord" we can look past the day-to-day politics, disputes, personal attacks, and any other distractions and see that our ultimate reward is not a paycheck, a promotion, personal recognition, stock options, a more powerful position, or any other form of financial or worldly recognition. Rather, our reward is a powerful yet simple, "Well done, my good and faithful servant," from our heavenly Father as we receive that inheritance of eternal life from him.

Of course, some might take this to mean Christians should take the most menial of servant roles. But that is not the case at all. While our daily attitudes should be servantlike, Christians shouldn't be embarrassed or hesitant to aspire to greater and more significant roles. While we should be content in whatever role or position we find ourselves, we should also be happy to seek to gain positions of influence and use those for God's kingdom. Think of the great men of the Bible: Joseph, second in command to the greatest earthly leader of the time, Pharaoh; Moses, son of Pharaoh, leader of the Hebrew nation; Daniel, second in command to three different kings of a dominating world power; Nehemiah, trusted advisor to his king; and David and Solomon, leaders of the greatest nation on earth in their day. Over and over we see men of God in positions of greatness and influence. In many cases, I see that the lack of Christian leaders in different fields such as media or politics has led to drifts away from Christian and moral principles. As a U.S. citizen we can look proudly upon the fact that almost all of the Founding Fathers of our nation were solid, churchgoing Christians. When the thought of separation of church and state was raised, it was so that the church would not be a state church like the Church of England had become. Such a thought was never meant to keep people's faith away from our nation or our political views (recall "In God We Trust"). Oh, may God Almighty today see in us a nation that chooses to honor him. May we be a nation that God can, in fact, bless.

We read in the popularized prayer of Jabez:

Jabez cried out to the God of Israel, "Oh, that you would bless me and enlarge my territory! Let your hand be with me, and keep me from harm so that I will be free from pain." And God granted his request. (1 Chron. 4:10)

He clearly sought the Lord's blessing on his life and possessions, but with God's hand on him, guiding his every step. I pray this prayer often: Oh Lord, enlarge my territory that I could be an increasingly powerful witness for your kingdom. Oh Lord, enlarge my possessions so that I may give greater support to the work of your kingdom here on earth. Oh Lord, use whatever position I am in at work, home, or in the community to lead people to you through my life and witness.

BALANCING WORK AND REST

Over my career, as described in chapter 1, I've had some intense periods of hard work. When we were completing the 80486 chip design, for example, our lives consisted of this: Work maybe eighteen to twenty hours, go home, sleep a bit, shower, and be back in six to eight hours for another eighteen to twenty hours. We were working around the clock, every day of the week. We were in a race against the industry, our internal schedule, and of course the challenges we established for ourselves.

We had committed to upper management to be done by Christmas 1988. Well, December 25 came and went, and while we were working at a feverish pace, the chip wasn't yet complete. New Year's Day came and went. We labored through January and into February. The days and hours continued to build in intensity and pressure. During this intense period as we were working toward design completion, a team member came wandering into my office. As he sort of stumbled in, he muttered in somewhat incoherent and fractured sentences about a problem with the chip. Clearly, this fellow was on the verge of burnout and needed a break, quick.

After the climax of tapeout was thankfully completed and we were waiting for the first samples back from fabrication, we took immediate and drastic action. Except for a skeleton crew, we kicked people out of the building and insisted they take some well-earned rest and relaxation. If they weren't part of the skeleton crew, they weren't to be found in the building for three weeks, or until the first test silicon had returned from the fabrication facility, whichever came first.

Maybe we can refer to this as "managed intensity." We need to balance periods of great focus and work—of being the best and applying huge portions of our time to our careers—with times for rest, relaxation, family, and vacations.

Working hard while prioritizing God and family is much like the juggling act I referred to earlier. While work demands, church demands, and personal time are clamoring for our attention, the challenge and opportunity is to just do it. My wife and I have had more discussions about my schedule and the allocation and use of my time than anything else in our married life. On more than one occasion, these have developed into heated arguments.

Over ten years ago, we started a point system to keep track of how I am doing. This may sound a bit crazy, but it has helped us to not debate the data about how much I've been home. Instead, it has helped us to move more quickly to a positive discussion concerning what to do about how much I'm at home or traveling. Often, it isn't a discussion about the hours but rather her feeling of being alone. Sometimes it is a discussion that while I've been physically home, I've not really been there mentally or emotionally, having been distracted by work even when I'm in the house. If I'm answering e-mail to catch up on work at night, I'm still at work even if I'm physically at home.

Our system works like this: Days I'm home before 5:00 p.m. are worth two points; days I'm home before 6:15 p.m. are worth one point; and days I'm home after 6:15 p.m. or not home at all that evening are zero points. Weekend days that I'm away get minus one point. The sum of those points for the month is the numerator. The denominator is the number of work days for the month. At the end of each month, we compare the sum of these points with the number of work days in the month. My example below is for a twelve-month period. Vacations or holidays don't count (unless, of course, I'm traveling on any of those days in which case they count as minus one each).

2005	JAN	FEB	MAR	APR	MAY	JUN	JUL	AUG	SEP	OCT	NOV	DEC
LEAVE BEFORE 5 (2 PTS)	3	2	2	1	3	3	2	2	3	1	1	4
LEAVE BEFORE 6:15 (1 PT)	6	8	4	4	5	9	1	3	5	4	3	10
LEAVE AFTER 6:15 (0 PTS)	8	7	10	15	9	7	5	16	12	15	17	5
WEEKEND DAYS (-1 PT)	1			2				2		2	3	
TOTAL DAYS OF MONTH	17	17	16	20	17	19	8	21	20	20	21	19
TOTAL POINTS FOR MONTH	11	12	8	4	11	15	5	5	11	4	2	18
PERCENT FOR MONTH	65%	71%	50%	20%	65%	79%	63%	24%	55%	20%	10%	95%
12 MONTH RUNNING AVERAGE	64%	64%	67%	60%	57%	58%	57%	50%	50%	52%	50%	51%

This system has helped remove the emotion from our discussion of my time. Prior to instituting this system, we'd often have ineffective and frustrating conversations something like the following:

Linda: "You've been gone too much lately."

Pat: "No, I've actually been home more this last month than the prior."

Linda: "No, you haven't, this month has been much worse than the prior."

Pat: "Well, that's not really the case. Remember last week? I was home four out of five nights."

Linda: "But the week before you were gone four days and had some meetings on the weekend."

Pat: "No, that was last month."

Linda: "No, it wasn't."

Pat: "Yes, it was before our Mother's Day weekend celebration."

Linda: "No …"

While this system is far from perfect, it puts the data in front of both of us and allows us to focus on the real issues. As an engineer by training, my life is governed by what the data says. Yet if the data shows one thing but Linda's perception indicates otherwise, we need to discuss a different issue than mere "time." Perhaps I was home more but was not helping around the house or not taking the kids to and fro and letting Linda have some well-deserved quiet time. Then maybe I could adjust things and get this one from basketball practice and take that one to his hockey game and allow Linda to spend the entire evening without getting in the car. Other times, the data showed me that I had simply not kept a careful watch on my schedule and allowed meetings and other work to take over again.

A number of years ago, Linda and I had a discussion as I was getting home a little later a few more nights of the week and hitting the airport tarmac a few too many times a month. I then discussed it with my spiritual mentor, Bryce, whom I'll discuss a bit more in the next chapter. Finally, Linda and I sat down to address the situation at length.

While the conversation was difficult, we instituted some actions to improve my time at home. Now I make a high priority to leave work at 5:00 p.m. Monday through Thursday. I've made clear to my office and administrative assistant that 5:00 is my departure time on these days, except on rare occasions when there is simply an unavoidable meeting. I can still do a call on the cell phone as I make my drive home, but I'm getting into the car at 5:00. Further, to get an early start on the weekend, I leave by 4:00 p.m. on Fridays. To make the system work, I need to be very diligent and consistent on my expectations, because it is easy for items to come creeping onto my calendar after hours.

Linda and the kids don't care how early I start work in the morning; they are in bed anyway or getting ready for school. If I'm not going to the gym that morning, I will typically get into work at 6:00 a.m. or sometimes even earlier to stay on top of things. Also, after Linda and the kids have gone to bed at night, it doesn't matter to them how late I stay up working. However, it matters an awful lot how many hours I am home—really home and undistracted—between 5:00 or 6:00 p.m. and 9:00 or 10:00 p.m. during the week and on weekends (of course, as you get to teenagers, that might be till 1:00 a.m.!). Those are the special family hours and should be treated preciously. Each of us needs to put great priority on these evening hours as the prime time for family.

Of course, I'm still far from perfect. Sometimes I'll hide in the garage or take a swing around the block once before pulling into the driveway to finish that last important call. Also, after dinner when Linda and the kids have gotten involved in homework or on the computer or reading a book, it's very easy to slide back into my study. While I might start legitimately working on some item for the household, my computer feels like a magnet or gravitational pull to suck me back into work mode. Maybe an e-mail has come in that needs my attention, and a few minutes later, I'm engrossed in my work again.

Also, being a goal-oriented individual, it's great to work toward a target. Using this system, my goal with Linda has been 70 percent on the "at home" chart. You and your spouse should probably take a sampling of how you are doing under normal circumstances and then choose a goal for the future. While it might seem trivial, a goal can be a powerful thing—and of course, pick a reward for meeting the goal to build even more enthusiasm for your efforts.

While this system is far from perfect, having a data-driven approach to time management takes much of the emotion out of your discussions. You'll also find earning some points will motivate you to simply do a better job of getting and being at home.

WORK/FAMILY CONFLICTS

Of course, this idea of managed intensity won't come easily and on many occasions will come under intense pressure as you try to balance work and family time. Sometimes this pressure will come from your own desires to be successful in your career. Other times it will arise from your boss or directly from demands of the workplace, where you will be asked to step up to a higher level, stay late, or push out a family commitment.

A few years ago, I was in charge of a project that was to be launched at PC Expo in New York City. PC Expo typically fell in mid-June, right after the kids got out of school. Unfortunately, before the venue and date were confirmed for the product launch, we as a family had decided to take the first two weeks after school as our yearly vacation time. We had made some extensive vacation plans, and not only would it have been difficult to change them, but it would have also been a big disappointment to the rest of the family. All of a sudden, a huge conflict of family and work was under way.

To make matters worse, this was a high-visibility project in the company. Further, Intel's president, Andy Grove, held a personal interest in the project. Despite these added pressures, and determined to live by my priorities, I decided that I would keep the commitment to my family vacation. I worked to prepare other capable folks to handle the launch in my absence.

When Andy learned of my plans, he was disappointed and communicated that displeasure on multiple occasions both privately and publicly. If you'd ever met Andy, you'd understand the intensity his communications can take. I was in the doghouse, and everyone knew it. Despite the escalating pressure, I decided to take the family vacation and ask someone else in my group to handle the product announcement. To make matters even worse, the launch of the new category of products was less than perfect, and one of our largest customers became upset with Intel in the process. With this miscue added to my perceived sin of prioritization, my office suddenly felt like a Siberian kennel.

Clearly, part of this very cold winter feeling was my own doing. The launch didn't go well, and I should have done more in making certain everything was arranged for perfection before I left. The bigger issue, though, was that I had made a firm decision to prioritize family vacation over work. Reflecting on the period, except for better preparation, I'd make the same decisions all over again.

On many other occasions, I've chosen conference calls over flying to be face-to-face for a meeting. Sometimes I'll prepare other managers to cover meetings for me. Other times I may not stay late to finish a particular project. While I like to squeeze in a few calls on my commute home at night, I know that if I'm still on the phone when I walk in the door, I'm sending a clear message to Linda and the kids: I'm still at work. I bow out of numerous opportunities to entertain or to spend time socializing after work. On other occasions I've said no to taking on an extra project that might have helped me to win credits toward a promotion or raise. One time, Andy Grove offered me to be his technical assistant. This was a pretty lucrative position. Corporate-wide visibility could be expected as a result of sitting in the office of the president and CEO, and leadership qualities would develop by working with him on a daily basis. Several of Intel's leaders used this position as a key transition point for their careers. Knowing that it would systematically have me away from home four or five days of the week and after a brief discussion with Linda, I declined.

Conflicts will come, and storms will arise. However, if you've developed a clear reputation for being a hard worker and a great employee, you can weather them effectively. Not only will you weather them, but your character will also grow, and your reputation and credibility will increase through the process. If you are intensely committed to the company's success and doing your best in all situations—even ones where you may not like your job, peers, or supervisors—you can live by your principles and still achieve a lot of success.

On the one hand, you need to make the commitments and trade-offs to do nothing but a great job, to engage in those periods of intensity with your total commitment and focus. Doing that, however, requires and allows you to balance those periods with times of rest and vacation.

Working hard and being a great employee over an extended period will build a stronger and stronger reputation for you at your place of employment. Think of it like an invisible bank account of long-term value to your employer. If you have worked hard and shown great dedication to the company, you will be well positioned to handle the turbulent times as they arise; I promise you, they will come. Practically speaking, there are always difficulties. Spiritually speaking, Satan will not allow a man or woman of principle to emerge without more than a few challenges to the person's decisions and choices.

In fact, everyone who wants to live a godly life in Christ Jesus will be persecuted. (2 Tim. 3:12)

For instance, suppose you've been one of the top-ranked employees over many years. You've gone the extra mile on programs critical to the company; you've shown unswerving ethics and consistent loyalty. Consequently, you will have created a value account of great positive merit on your behalf. Then a situation like the PC Expo example arises. While the company may not be pleased with the trade-off you are making in this particular instance, this situation would be considered in the overall context of your employment. And the large positive balance you have in this invisible value account easily covers this withdrawal.

Suppose, on the other hand, that you've had continual second thoughts about this company. You've done well at times, but during other periods you've had questionable performance. You've conflicted with different supervisors, doing well with some but poorly with others. You've also had accusations of inappropriate behavior or challenging the ethics of your supervisors. In this case, lacking a strong and consistent reputation for being a great employee, tough situations will be difficult if not impossible to weather. Some instance will arise where you desperately want to make good on a commitment to your family, but your value account at work is already in a deficit. Making another withdrawal will put you firmly into bankruptcy court, jeopardizing your long-term career growth and possibly your job.

On two occasions following my PC Expo conflict, I was again faced with a choice between a family vacation commitment and a work commitment. In one case, our family plans were flexible and—unlike the PC Expo case—we didn't have extensive plans. I sought but couldn't find a suitable replacement for the work assignment. Given the flexibility in the family situation, I took a day out of my vacation and kept the work commitment.

In the other instance, our family plans were set, and again I made the decision to keep my commitment to the family time. This case wasn't as visible or significant as the PC Expo example, but it was still a visible decision to live by my priorities and put family first.

I encourage you not to be simply dogmatic in either direction. Applying these principles in the various circumstances you will face can be challenging. Sometimes your choice will be clear; other times, judging whether you can afford to keep the family commitment will prove difficult, if not impossible.

· · · · ·

Yes, we're to the point where you can clearly see the juggling act at work. Conflicts between work, family, and God lie squarely in front of us. A consistent and strong reputation can carry you through many challenges. If you've made it this far, you are making strong progress toward becoming a master juggler. However, making these gray-area judgment calls requires learning, prayer, and wisdom, and having a few other wise heads around you won't hurt either—which is the subject of our next chapter.

• • • • •

CHAPTER 5 QUESTIONS

1. How do you handle work commitments that come into conflict with family commitments?

2. How can you manage when projects become intense and short target dates are set—when it becomes difficult to please family and friends while still being an effective employee?

3. In an environment where corruption is a way to achieve goals, how can one maintain integrity?

4. Would you continue to work hard even if you came across unethical behavior in your company?

5. A bad economy puts a lot of pressure in our work lives. Where should one draw the line in terms of commitments and responsibilities?

6. How do you see the trade-off between working to fill the pockets of another individual and earning a living for yourself?

7. How often do you review your time chart?

6

· · · · ·

Developing Mentor Relationships

· · · · ·

AT A LATE STAGE of the 80386 design, I gave a presentation to upper-level management at Intel. I had gone from being a technician to being an entry-level engineer. I was doing great on the project and was receiving promotions every year. I managed a few technicians and had gained credibility and increasingly responsible roles within the design team. However, I was still quite junior and largely unknown to most of the upper management at Intel. I had made it past private first class but not too much further in my career progression. At this point in time, I was directly in charge of the tapeout process for the 80386. For multiple years individuals in the team had been working in seclusion on their portions of the chip. As mentioned earlier, tapeout is the assembly of those pieces into the complete database and then sending the design database to fabrication for the first chips.

The point of my presentation was that because of serious,

persistent problems with our computer systems, disaster loomed on the horizon. We might never be able to finish the chip. This created a buzz of controversy, but I stood by my data and assertion and insisted that we urgently escalate the matter with our mainframe supplier to get the issues resolved.

One day about a week after this meeting, I was huddled comfortably in my office, intently working on a portion of the design. Wrapped up in my own little world of problems, ideas, and design, it might have taken a cannon blast to bring me back to the surrounding environment. Instead, all it took was the loud blast of the ring of my desk phone.

I had absolutely no desire to be disturbed and was annoyed at this blast of bells. After several rings, which didn't stop despite my reluctance to answer, I picked up the phone to hush the annoying ring. In the most annoyed, disturbed, and sarcastic voice I could muster, I demanded, "Who is it?"

The response was a baritone "Andy."

To which I, attempting to outdo the sarcasm of my initial greeting, bellowed, "Andy who!?"

The response came back quickly, "Andy Grove."

I almost died on the spot. I was more flustered and embarrassed than any other time I can recall. This was *the* Andy Grove. Founder of the company. Later to become *Time* magazine's Man of the Year. President and soon to become CEO of the company. Andy, undaunted, described how he had been impressed by my presentation the other day. He wanted to know my career plans at the company.

I gave a very weak reply, barely able to form a coherent sentence, much less a good response. Undeterred, he began shelling me with rapid-fire questions: What are your goals? What do you read? What are you studying? What do you want your next job to be? Having started in a flustered state, I could barely form adequate sentences in response.

Following a few of these strong questions from him and my very weak responses, he replied, "Those are lousy answers. Be in my office within two weeks with better ones."

He was right about my answers. I had been startled by his call and entirely unprepared for his line of questioning. Besides, other than "being an engineer," I hadn't considered what I wanted to accomplish. My only goal was to be the engineer telling the technician what to do. Now I was faced with a dilemma: I either show up in the president's office or leave the country! Fortunately, I got past my huge embarrassment, arranged for time a couple of weeks later, and went with trepidation to Andy's office to discuss my career and development goals. This began an ad hoc mentoring relationship that lasts to this day. As he would see weaknesses or problems in my character, or as I would be struggling with certain areas or issues, I'd get some time on his calendar, and he would offer his wealth of experience, genius, and expertise to this young and ambitious soul. Among other things, as mentioned earlier, he trained me to broaden my reading interests to include staples like the *Wall Street Journal,* and he helped me to sharpen my career goals.

I still reflect on this experience and say, "Wow!" Andy reached numerous layers down in the organization and tapped upon me with interest. As president of the company, he was of course incredibly busy. Also, he was surrounded by other aspiring and capable individuals. I was humbled but also extraordinarily motivated by his interest in my career. I listened studiously to his guidance. I might question his comments, challenge them enough so that I really understood, but never would I dismiss them without deep and careful thought.

Over the years, as I've tried to emulate Andy's mentoring activities, nothing disappoints me more than someone I am mentoring who will not accept my counsel. Not that anyone should simply take a mentor's advice and implement it blindly. But, a mentor's feedback should be consumed, pondered deeply, and in most cases put into practice with specific action plans. To be mentored, you must have a teachable spirit. I just met with an individual recently who spent almost all our time justifying his actions and worth. After speaking bluntly with him, I came away quite convinced spending more time mentoring this individual wasn't a good use of my time or his.

> The way of a fool seems right to him, but a wise man listens to advice (Prov. 12:15).

I recall one mentoring session with Andy where he had some particularly tough messages for me. I listened intently, fed back to him clearly what he said, and described my initial thoughts on how I'd explore them. Andy was impressed that I was embracing his feedback so well despite the tough messages. Through Andy, God was slowly developing a more teachable spirit in me.

I've been extraordinarily blessed to have some wonderful mentors and teachers in my career. I've worked with some of the finest in the industry. I've been counseled by the greatest technologist of semiconductors, Gordon Moore; mentored by the greatest strategist, Andy Grove; guided by one of the greatest operational managers,

Craig Barrett. I've met and worked with household names like Bill Gates, Larry Ellison, Michael Dell, and Steve Jobs. As a leader in our field, I get to interact with many of the best and brightest throughout the high-tech industry.

Through my experience with Andy, I began to understand the idea of "mentors" in a deep and profound way. We can see it in Scripture:

> Two are better than one, because they have a good return for their work: If one falls down, his friend can help him up. But pity the man who falls and has no one to help him up! Also, if two lie down together, they will keep warm. But how can one keep warm alone? Though one may be overpowered, two can defend themselves. A cord of three strands is not quickly broken. (Eccl. 4:9–12)

I love that last line: A cord of three strands is not quickly or, in some translations, easily, broken. Sometimes events and difficulties arise that we simply don't have the capacity to handle using our own wisdom, abilities, or strength. But through our relationships and particularly our mentors, we "aren't quickly broken." Jesus provided that kind of relationship to his twelve disciples, and even more intimately with his inner three. We see other examples in Scripture, like when Paul takes the great apostle Peter aside and rebukes him (Gal. 2:11). We see Paul with his band of young disciples in Timothy, Titus, and others. We see Paul working alongside Barnabas as a peer. In letter after letter of the New Testament, we see Paul take these individuals he's mentoring and passionately and lovingly guide them.

MULTIPLE MENTORS

It's often beneficial to have multiple mentors in our lives. Our spiritual mentor may not be the same person we need for our career or professional mentor. We might also have certain areas of our lives where we need a mentor who is specifically strong or capable in that area.

Maybe you're struggling with how to be a better spouse; you should seek a mentor who is particularly strong in that area. Choose someone whose relationships with his or her children and spouse are the kind you want for yourself and for your family.

Maybe you need to work on a certain skill set in your work life, like time management. You should seek a mentor who has demonstrated ability in planning and in managing his or her life with discipline and order.

Let me also encourage you to pursue at least three levels of mentoring relationships: a mentor, a peer, and a mentee. Scripturally, you can compare this to having a Paul in your life, a Barnabas, and finally a Timothy. While a direct biblical connection is definitely stretching the Scripture, in my own mind I liken these three with the "three strands" of Ecclesiastes 4:12.

First, you need someone you are being mentored by, like Paul was to Timothy or Titus. This should be someone you can look up to and respect. Someone who has capabilities and experiences you haven't yet mastered. Someone who is accomplished and mature in areas you desire to grow in. You also need someone who is willing and committed to investing in your life. Finally, that person needs to be eager to see you grow and succeed. For many years, this is the role that Andy Grove played in my professional career.

But you know that Timothy has proved himself, because as a son with his father he has served with me in the work of the gospel. (Phil. 2:22)

Second, you need a peer, someone you can be a deep friend, buddy, or pal with. Paul and Barnabas had this kind of relationship. You need someone who isn't too impressed by you, who is ready to tell you the truth. Someone who sees you enough to observe your successes and your mistakes and isn't afraid to tell you about them. Paul filled this role for Peter at least once in his life. Envision this interaction as described by Paul:

When Peter came to Antioch, I opposed him to his face, because he was clearly in the wrong. Before certain men came from James, he used to eat with the Gentiles. But when they arrived, he began to draw back and separate himself from the Gentiles because he was afraid of those who belonged to the circumcision group. (Gal. 2:11–12)

That seems like an Intel meeting to me—not meant to create strife, but direct and very blunt when something doesn't seem quite right. Maybe you can recall a few similar instances at your place of employment.

Given my strong personality, finding a peer has been hard for me over the years. I'm not particularly open about my feelings, and I don't find many people whom I don't overwhelm and yet I trust and respect. I was saddened when one peer moved to Kenya to be a missionary. It had taken me too long to find one, and now I needed to travel halfway around the world to see him.

Third, you need someone to whom you are passing your life's experiences—a Timothy. Someone you can teach, tutor, and encourage. Someone in whose growing maturity you take joy.

As a manager for many years, I've picked a few people to mentor in whom I saw potential and thought they could benefit from what I've learned. I've taken great pleasure in seeing some of them making it to positions of director, vice president, or fellow. What a joy it is to see those you've invested in make it to positions of success and influence, knowing you helped them get there.

FINDING MENTORS

As I've given this talk over the years, I've been asked numerous times, how do you find a mentor, or do they find you? Well, I'm sorry to tell you that I've found no simple formula. Much of it is simply the right interpersonal chemistry. Not being a psychologist, I can't describe why some relationships work great and others don't. However, I can identify a few critical characteristics of a good mentor. I think there are three:

1. Trust and respect—you need someone whom you have a genuine respect for; you'll naturally value the person's opinions and what he or she has to say. You need someone you can trust—someone you are comfortable telling about your deepest feelings, sins and failures, and emotions. Similarly, for the people you are mentoring, they need that of you.

2. Character and capabilities—your mentor should have

capabilities you want to learn. If a course catalog for a class advertised that the teacher had never actually done what he was going to talk about but he'd read up on it really well, would you attend? Of course not. You want to learn from a master. Similarly in your mentor, you want someone who has skill and experience in those areas where you wish to improve in your own life.

3. Time and commitment—while it may not require a huge amount of time, mentoring does demand a commitment. It might be just an hour or two every month or so. Or you might be in a period of your life when mentoring is more critical and you need to meet much more frequently— maybe once per week.

Finding a mentor can be challenging. Sometimes, as in the case of Andy Grove with me, a mentor will seek you out. May God grant you such good fortune.

I suggest, however, that you don't just wait for someone to ask you. Go broach the subject with a person you'd like as a mentor. Say something like, "As I'm growing and learning, I see the value a mentor could play in my life. I've been impressed by what you've done with your life, and you have some skills and knowledge I could really benefit from. Can I talk with you about possibly becoming a mentor to me?"

I recall one summer several years ago when a college student doing an internship at Intel approached me in this manner. I was not only somewhat flattered, but I also gained an immediate respect for the young man. He sought to better himself, and he was eager to find people who might help. He had done his homework, knowing a good bit about me, my career, and my faith. He was also well prepared with a list of questions he wanted to discuss with me. I became quickly convinced that any time I spent with him would be a good investment of my energy.

Seeking out your Timothy is another matter. Imagine an aspiring young person getting a call from you where you say something like "I've watched you, and you have talent. I enjoy watching you grow and develop. I'd like to invest some of my life's experiences and wisdom into your life. Can we get together sometime and talk about it?" I've never heard of such a call being rebuffed, even if the two of you eventually decide you're not the right fit for each other.

Finally, how do you recruit a Barnabas? You might say something like "I could really use someone to get together with and confidentially share our concerns and weaknesses. I'd like an accountability partner who would commit to meet and pray with me periodically. I don't know if you have the time or desire for this, but if we could get together to discuss the possibility sometime, I'd really appreciate it."

As noted above, sometimes you need a mentor in a specific area of your life. You might mentor him in some ways and be mentored by him in others.

A close friend, Bryce Jessup, is the man who married Linda and me twenty-five years ago. Over the years, we have stayed in close contact. Bryce is well regarded in the area of marriage and family, and over the years I've continued to use him as a mentor in these areas. At the same time, Bryce has found me valuable as his "vision" mentor. As president of William Jessup University (WJU; formerly known as San Jose Christian College), he needs to set a direction and paint a vision for the staff, supporters, board, and student body. I've been able to challenge him to think bigger, to see a greater God, and to seek the potential areas where God could enlarge his work. Given my business experience, I've also helped him learn how to engage with businessmen and include them in his work and vision. Thus, we've mentored each other in these different areas.

I recall one occasion a few years ago when I was serving as a board member for WJU. I was in from out of town for the board meeting, and he offered me a room at his house for the night. With some trepidation, he asked me if he could share his vision for the college. I said, "Sure. Fire away." He jumped right in and went on for five-plus minutes. He described his ideas for the campus physical property, for new programs for students, and for growth in the student body. He discussed a few longer-range ideas he had as well. When he finished, he eagerly asked what I thought.

With little hesitation, I gave him a single-word reply: "Wimpy." I felt strongly led to challenge him to a greater and bolder vision for the college. My God was greater than the picture he was painting, and I was certain he would and could use the college in a more powerful way.

Bryce was immediately crushed and defeated by my quick and harsh critique. However, this prompting eventually led Bryce to a much more aggressive plan for the college. Bryce has probably told this story a hundred times since that occasion. While I had burst his bubble, this conversation was quite the divine appointment. God had much bigger plans for Bryce and the college, and I was God's voice delivering the message that evening. The college subsequently relocated from an ugly, landlocked, run-down campus in central San Jose to a spacious property with enormous room for growth in Rocklin, California. They moved from a location where the city council had zero support for them to a county that embraced them with warm and supportive arms. They changed the name from San Jose Christian College to William Jessup University (www.jessup.edu). The student body has grown rapidly. They are seeking to become the premier Christian university in Northern California. Today, Bryce is absolutely passionate for the Lord's work, and the vision he has for the university is energizing. He's more confident than ever of God's leading and direction in his ministry. Though he has reached an age at which many would consider retirement, he's launching maybe the most productive period of his long and effective ministry. This is the kind of thing that mentors will do for each other, challenging and encouraging each other to do greater things and become greater individuals for God's work. While they love the other person just the way he or she is, they are eager to see the person improve and accomplish greater things professionally and spiritually.

This example also allows me to make another point. Generally, a mentor is someone you'd consider older than yourself. With age comes experience and wisdom. The Bible clearly teaches us to honor age. Don't treat age as a firm requirement, however, as you go about picking your Paul, Timothy, and Barnabas. While I won't point out how much older Bryce is than I am, it brings me a certain pleasure when he refers to me as his mentor.

· · · · ·

As we've gone through this discussion, I've generally presented mentoring as a specific and ongoing relationship. But you will find that many ad hoc situations arise in which you might be mentored or be able to mentor someone else. One friend of mine at Intel, Will, often passes me a casual note in a meeting or a gesture when he sees me venturing into challenging subjects. Likewise, I will advise him when I see areas in his life that he might be able to improve. On one occasion before a particularly difficult presentation, Will took me aside a few minutes beforehand and encouraged me to acknowledge the others who had participated in this material's preparation. He also cautioned me to emphasize the primary point I needed to make without getting stuck on some of the other important but potentially distracting items. The presentation went exceptionally well, and Will's timely advice was quite valuable.

On another occasion, I noticed that Will became defensive at moments of great stress in meetings. His reactions were too emotional, leading others to disregard his valuable input. I advised him and helped him overcome this weakness, leading to a significant increase in his effectiveness. Over the years, our casual and off-cuff mentoring has proven valuable for both of us. At one point Andy Grove complimented me on the improvements he saw in Will as a direct result of my mentoring him.

• • • • •

In one difficult real-estate transaction, I've advised a close friend on how he might handle the myriad issues in both negotiations as well as legal matters. In yet another situation, I've encouraged the head of a church-planting organization to be more aggressive and take the ministry to a greater level of national and international impact and results. He has done so, and today Stadia has a national agenda and is beginning a look at international fields as well.

By the same token, in recent years I've been counseled in overcoming some difficulties I've had in professional interpersonal relationships. While I had taken steps to address them, the same kinds of comments had shown up in my performance reviews for probably the last fifteen years. Some specific and focused mentoring in these areas has resulted in breakthroughs that many have recognized. One person commented to me a couple of years ago, "I like the new Pat."

While some companies offer specific mentoring programs, to me the critical aspects of mentoring do not come from a program. The keys are, first, finding an individual with the right skills and interpersonal relationship; and second, deciding to better yourself based on the advice of this person.

Finally, a few words of warning are in order. A mentoring relationship is deeply personal. You'll be sharing the depths of your character, emotions, desires, and secrets. Confidentiality is crucial. That expectation and commitment to each other should be spelled out and agreed to up front. I've never been badly burned by a mentoring-related indiscretion, but some things I considered private have been spread to others. Even the slightest indiscretion can lead to distrust, which will permanently render the mentoring relationship ineffectual.

Another potential danger is simple neglect. One or both parties just don't have the time to invest in the relationship, or maybe it's just not working, but the person feeling that way is afraid to say so. The fact is, though, that not every relationship will go well. Honest communication and a willingness either to find answers or move on are needed.

Despite those potential pitfalls, as we close our discussion on mentors, once again my simple advice mimics the Nike slogan "Just Do It." Get past any embarrassment you might have over making yourself vulnerable to another person in this way. We men are typically reluctant to have these types of deep relationships. For many years my wife, Linda, ran the women's mentoring program at our church. Ladies just love the social aspect of getting together. Often we men are reluctant to make the continued investment in our time and energy. However, the Bible clearly encourages us to "just do it":

> Do not rebuke a mocker or he will hate you; rebuke a wise man and he will love you. Instruct a wise man and he will be wiser still; teach a righteous man and he will add to his learning. (Prov. 9:8–9)

If my own life, or any of the many I've encouraged in this area, is any indication, you'll find immense benefit from weaving your life together with those of your Timothy, Barnabas, and Paul: your "three strands." You will not be easily broken if you develop these relationships to support, help, and guide you. Hopefully this is an encouragement and starting point to your "three strands," and you can find further insight in some other valuable materials.[6]

• • • • •

CHAPTER 6 QUESTIONS

1. How might you go about finding a mentor?

2. What should you do in your mentoring time? How often should you meet?

3. What do you think about having more than one mentor? How many mentors should one have?

4. How can you mentor team members at work or employees that report to you?

5. Can you think of three people who would make good "Paul," "Timothy," and "Barnabas" roles in your life? Write down their names and commit to approach them about a mentoring relationship as the first step to weave your life together with theirs.

7

. . . . .

Living Authentically
as a Clear Witness

. . . . .

ONE TIME, SHORTLY AFTER my promotion to vice president at Intel, I took a business trip that had me flying cross-country. I found myself sitting next to a woman I hadn't met before, and we started chatting. When she asked about my work and I described my responsibilities, role at Intel, and some areas of recent successes, she seemed intrigued.

When I reciprocated and asked about her work, she explained that she was the editor-in-chief for the parent company of our local Portland-area newspaper and told me some of what that involved. After a bit, she asked the leading question of what I thought of the Portland paper.

I explained to her that the local paper had earned a reputation for an anti-Christian bias, portraying Christians as unintelligent and weak in character. There had been several recent editorial-page articles that were most offensive, raising more than a bit of raucousness in the Christian community. I took the opportunity to say politely that I found the bias not only personally offensive as a Christian, but also to be poor journalism and bad business practice on the part of the paper.

The woman was surprised if not shocked by my direct response. To her credit she took my concerns seriously. Given I had already established my credibility with her in my earlier conversation, she took my comments seriously. In a subsequent exchange of letters, she indicated not only her intent to investigate but also to address the concerns I raised.

If you've made it this far and have begun implementing the first five principles I've suggested, you should be ready for this next step in your journey: being a clear witness. If you've started making significant changes in your family, your work, and personal priorities, people will likely notice and say things like "Hey, why are you leaving earlier at night?" or "Why aren't you golfing with us on Sundays anymore?" or "I noticed you reading something the other day."

As these questions are thrown at you, how will you answer? Will you shyly deflect their interest with something like "It's nothing, just trying to improve myself a bit"? Or will you respectfully but truthfully declare your relationship with God and your conviction to live a more balanced life applying his principles?

> Whoever acknowledges me before men, I will also acknowledge him before my Father in heaven. But whoever disowns me before men, I will disown him before my Father in heaven. (Matt. 10:32–33)

This passage makes it clear that the answer to those seemingly minor or innocuous questions can have dramatic implications.

Will we use them as springboards to share our lives and faith with another?

Far too often, we seem afraid or nervous to tell the truth. We'll duck the question or get embarrassed or tell a little lie—if there is such a thing. But let me challenge you to give the straightforward answer and to be nothing but God's bold man or woman in those situations. When someone asks, "Why don't you golf on Sundays?" respectfully and earnestly answer, "I've decided to prioritize my relationship with God, and I've committed to being in church. Also, I've decided I want my kids to see me being the spiritual leader of our household. I want to lead the way, and I want each of them to be learning from my example."

When you become a clear and visible witness, two powerful things happen. First, you've identified yourself publicly as a Christian. No shyness, no apologies, and no more closet Christianity. You've declared yourself a disciple of Christ. You have taken his name as your own.

Second, you've just made yourself accountable to the people to whom you've identified yourself. Every time you are in that person's presence, you will now have to live up to a certain standard. You've created a set of expectations that will be reminders to you whenever you are out and about. As you become a clear witness to two, three, ten, twenty, or more individuals who see you at work, home, and play, all of a sudden you've developed a network of implied accountability. They are watching you, and you know it.

In a short time, you will find you don't have any situations where you don't have some level of character accountability around you. This becomes a powerful tool to keep you on the right track. For example, once you've made it clear that you don't profane because of your position in Christ, you can't be careless about it in the future because others are now ready to respond. I'm now well known for not drinking alcohol, and I have a network of many in the factory, in the field, and among our customers who know my stand. My reputation goes before me in many settings, and I know I have to live up to the expectations and standard that I've created.

STEPPING OUT IN FAITH

Several years ago I was in a meeting with Andy Grove, and at one point he let loose a string of profanity to convey his dissatisfaction with something. His taking my Lord's name in vain didn't sit right with me, and I felt the Spirit compelling me to take action. Further, Andy is such a great man in so many regards that I felt he decreased his own image by resorting to such outbursts. I really didn't want to confront him on this matter. However, I couldn't quite shake this prompting from the Holy Spirit. As reluctant as I was, I decided I just needed to talk to him about it.

With prayer and thoughtful preparation, I took him aside and privately said in the most respectful manner possible: "Andy, I would really appreciate it if you might avoid such profanities. I find them offensive and would just ask that you consider trying not to take my Lord's name in vain." What kind of crazy thing was I doing even suggesting such a thing? He's the big boss, a founder, president, board member. He can do whatever he likes, including firing me!

Well, to my surprise and delight, he responded receptively,

saying, "You're right. Eva [Andy's wife] has been after me about this for many years. I'll work on it." Wow—you couldn't fathom my relief to his positive response!

A few weeks later I was at an Intel function that Eva also attended. She purposely found me in the crowd. After greeting me, she quickly stated, "Thank you. Thank you!" My mind was racing ... what was the president's wife thanking me for? She continued, "I've been after Andy for his profanity for many years. Thank you for challenging him on this!" For many years after that, if Andy and I were in a meeting together and he slipped into profanity, he'd make eye contact knowingly, confirming that he recognized the slip and reaffirming his accountability to me in this area.

I'm sure you'll find some hard-core profaners who wouldn't respond with as much respect, receptivity, and dignity as Andy did, but I've had the same little talk with probably a hundred or more people over the years, and every one of them has given me at least a respectful response. I don't attack their character or habit; rather I just phrase my request in a most courteous manner. "I would appreciate it if you wouldn't take my Lord's name in vain." I haven't demanded them to consider him Lord. I haven't condemned their behavior. I've just made a personal entreaty to them about my Lord and the use of his name when I'm present.

· · · · ·

A few years ago at Intel, a policy was instituted establishing employee-support groups. The first of these was Globe, the Gay and Lesbian support group. While many were upset by the existence of such an entity, a few saw an opportunity to take advantage of the same policy and sought to use it to God's glory. Shortly thereafter the Intel Bible Christian Network (IBCN) was initiated. The policy was for any employee-support group to meet as long as it satisfied certain broad guidelines.

As they were getting IBCN off the ground, they desired to have a public kickoff event, and I was asked to speak. I was concerned that this was too visible a role for an executive of the company to take. I also felt that if I did agree to speak, I needed to give an accurate and complete account of my Christian faith. After pondering, praying, and consulting a few others, I agreed. To several audiences of several hundred each, I gave the first talk on "Juggling God, Family, and Work, Work, Work."

The speech was extremely well received and led to a second, third, and fourth delivery of "Juggling" at other IBCN campus kickoff events. All of a sudden, I was exposing my Christian beliefs to hundreds of people inside the company.

As a result, many people became actively involved with IBCN. Several others were encouraged to be more open about their own faith. The most beneficial result, though, was that several other senior individuals in the company began stepping forward to identify themselves publicly as Christians. Being a clear witness was not only contagious but in this case multiplicative, as well.

BEING A CLEAR WITNESS IS NOT WITHOUT RISK

Many years ago when I was a junior engineer working on a portion of the 80386 design, another very senior engineer named Ed was working on another part of the chip. He was an avowed and vocal atheist. As we came to know of each other's strong views, Ed began to take me on as his personal target of assault. It was as if Ed were trying to revitalize the ancient Roman persecution of the Christians in the Colosseum, and I was the main event. He became increasingly extreme in his private and public attacks on me.

Never being one to be quiet or passive when attacked, I began sending him daily Scripture and devotions via e-mail in response to each of his assertions. But my scriptural proofs seemed to incite him all the more.

As this episode escalated and became increasingly public, an amazing thing occurred. Others of faith in the department, without encouragement or coaxing, began to stand up on my behalf. All of a sudden, people in restrooms and hallways would tell me that Ed was getting carried away, and they would describe their own beliefs and encourage me to remain strong in the face of these attacks.

While this experience was a far cry from the martyrdom of the first, second, and third centuries, or that which occurs today in some countries taking violent stands against Christians, I was left with a fresh perspective on how persecution can be good for the individual and also for the community of believers. When lax and comfortable, our faith will wax, wane, and wobble. When confronted, we must make a clear decision to respond or ignore. In this particular example, none of this could have occurred if I was unwilling to be a visible witness. By the way, while Ed eventually ceased his personal attacks on me, he also came to respect my convictions, and we became very good professional acquaintances. However, I don't know if any of the seeds I helped sow in his life ever led to any change in his spiritual status, and over the years I've lost track of him.

Now, as a senior person for the company, I'm often called upon to represent Intel, and I regularly find my values tested in peculiar ways. Intel is a great company and runs ongoing training programs to remain ethical and consistent with our stated values and policies. As the company has progressed and gone through certain difficult issues like the Pentium flaw experience, our firm ethical stance has become clearer and sharper.

In 1998, we had a situation with a customer called Intergraph. I was one of the principal senior managers involved from Intel. Unfortunately, the situation went from bad to worse, and Intergraph eventually filed a lawsuit against Intel for contractual violations, intellectual property infringement, and violation of antitrust laws. Mine was one of the few names from Intel specifically mentioned in the lawsuit.

You can only imagine the depth of introspection this case caused me. How often I replayed the various meetings with Intergraph executives in my mind. Had I acted ethically? Had I done everything in my power to avoid this situation? What might I have done differently?

As the lawsuit proceeded, a reporter with the *Wall Street Journal* interviewed me one day on a variety of technical topics. At one point he blurted out, "Since you are a Christian, Pat, I think yours will be the most interesting testimony of them all in the Intergraph lawsuit."

I'd had no idea that Dean, the reporter, knew I was a Christian, but somehow he learned of my faith. Further, while he expected other Intel employees to toe the company line, he expected me as a Christian to both tell the truth and be more forthcoming with the truth than other execs at Intel would be.

Well, the next day my Christian faith was being noted in the bible of the U.S. businessman, the *Wall Street Journal*. On the one hand, I was pleased to see my Christian faith noted publicly. However, to assert that it would lead me to confess things that non-Christians at Intel would not say was very troubling. Worse yet, some of the comments were taken by senior management in a negative way. They felt I had given the impression that Christian employees like myself were more ethical than non-Christians. As this example showed me, being a clear witness is not without its risks. But it's what we are called to be as men and women of faith.

PUTTING UP A WELCOME SIGN

I find that applying the principles in this book will create a reputation that will lead others to you in times of need. The husband of an administrative assistant in another department had cancer. The woman, whom I had not known previously, sought me out to let me know of the situation and to ask for my prayers.

A coworker's girlfriend suddenly died. In our next conversation, the man told me how my witness over the years had been an encouragement to him in his recent ordeal.

A few years ago, I received mail from Carl, a man who worked in my organization. He commented on how my witness was an ongoing challenge to him. In fact, he admitted to being quite negative about me if not slanderous. For many years, I haunted his thoughts and image of what a Christian was. Finally, many years after he had moved on from my organization, he became a Christian, citing my witness as a major influence in his life.

Imagine a conversation with a coworker in a time of medical or personal difficulty. You say, in the humblest and most empathetic of ways, "I'll be thinking of you and praying for you." Who, regardless of their faith, would not be encouraged by such a statement?

Of course, Scripture gives us the soundest reason of them all to be a clear witness:

> You are the light of the world. A city on a hill cannot be hidden. Neither do people light a lamp and put it under a bowl. Instead they put it on its stand, and it gives light to everyone in the house. In the same way, let your light shine before men, that they may see your good deeds and praise your Father in heaven. (Matt. 5:14–16)

Let me reiterate at this point that your job is the place where you are to be a great employee. Your desire to be a witness should not supersede the performance of your duties and responsibilities. You must first become and then continue to be a great employee. Only then and when circumstances arise that don't interfere with your work can you have an effective witness.

Some Christians spend so much time witnessing at work that they cease to be great employees. That's wrong, and it will erode their positions and reputations as employees. Such persistence, in turn, will hinder their credibility as witnesses. As with just about everything in this book, and most things in life, proper balance is the key.

I've had the opportunity to give this speech in a variety of situations while traveling with my job. While I'm in distant cities, Campus Crusade for Christ has been able to arrange speaking engagements where I can give my testimony and my juggling speech to businessmen and women, Christian groups, and men's meetings. I've enjoyed delivering this message, and I've even dusted off my juggling skills and used them as an object lesson. But while I enjoy the opportunities to speak, I agree to them only when they can be squeezed into my work schedule.

Intel does not fly me halfway around the world to be a wandering evangelist. They have me travel to get a job done, and I always challenge the Intel teams in the countries I visit to keep me entirely busy. With Intel employees worldwide I want to earn a reputation as a man who works hard for the company, giving it my very best in everything I do. However, as weekends or evenings might be open, I take the opportunities to again be a clear witness as part of those trips.

At one Campus Crusade event in India, a senior and well-known press person asked to interview me about my talk. I considered this a great opportunity and agreed. However, when the conversation became a discussion of Intel business, it became important to clarify my two distinct roles. I was speaking at this venue as an individual, not as an Intel executive. To discuss Intel business, we would have to use Intel's normal press channels and include Intel press relations as part of the interview as was our normal practice.

To be an effective witness in the workplace, you will need to learn and implement a clear separation of your position as a great employee (see chapter 5) and clear witness (as we've covered in this chapter). The Intergraph case and *Wall Street Journal* situation I described earlier was a learning experience for me. While I felt comfortable with my answers in the interview itself, seeing the reaction and how they came out in the press has led me to be much more precise about the clear separation between these two roles. I could have and should have in this case just stopped the interview, saying this is on these specific technical topics and as a result, I can't respond to these questions that discuss my personal faith. I failed to handle the inquiry properly, paid a price, and learned in the process.

Finally, being a clear witness will require you to keep your own skills sharp as a person of faith.

Preach the Word; be prepared in season and out of season; correct, rebuke and encourage—with great patience and careful instruction. (2 Tim. 4:2)

On one particular trip, the coworker I was traveling with was an atheist and was eager to challenge my clear witness with his own knowledge of the areas in the Bible that are hard to defend from a scientific perspective. He didn't easily back from a debate, and neither did I. By the time our flight was over, our debate was well known to the entire business class on the flight that day. In fact, a few of them even joined into the debate. Further, he did make some good points that I wasn't well prepared to answer. Thus, I was also challenged to study some of the many points he had made so I was better prepared in the future to give a defense for the hope that is in me.

It turned out that this man had been an officer in a local organization of atheists. Despite that debate, however, we had a cordial working relationship over the ensuing years until he retired from Intel. It doesn't appear as though he'll ever embrace Christianity, but I know he has heard the gospel at least once.

· · · · ·

As we've considered the key principles in this book, I trust that you can now see how applying them will build up your reputation and influence in the workplace, in your home, in your church, and in your community. You will be seen as a man or woman of character and proper priorities. And that standing will afford you numerous opportunities to be a clear and bold witness for Jesus Christ. In chapter 8, I'll discuss a few guidelines for how to better integrate your faith in your workplace and marketplace lives.

• • • • •

CHAPTER 7 QUESTIONS

1. How can you take opportunities to share God's Word at work? How would you do so? Are there any specific examples where you've been able to do so?

2. Under what circumstances would it be inappropriate to witness at your job?

3. What makes you uncomfortable in sharing your faith? What steps can you think of to help address those areas? Practice sharing your faith with your mentor or a Christian friend. Get to the point where you are comfortable with some simple discussion points about your faith.

4. If one is not a Christian, can he or she still go about bringing balance to life?

5. What are some practical situations that are going on in your life right now where you feel you should be a Christian witness but haven't had the courage to do so?

8

· · · · ·

Integrating Faith, Family, and Work

· · · · ·

A COUPLE OF YEARS ago I was approached by Intel HR that a number of complaints had arisen about my faith in the workplace. I was a very visible Intel executive with large organizational and strategic impact. There were some complaints related to some recent articles that were published that included interviews with me about my faith. The Intel IBCN network included a link to my mission statement from my personal Web site (www.patgelsinger.com). There were some complaints that the contents of my mission statement implied that I was biased toward Christians and, therefore, biased against those who were non-Christians. I was going to do some events in support of the launch of the simplified Chinese version of the first edition of this book in mainland China. The first edition of this book included "From the CTO of Intel Corporation" on the cover, which gave the appearance that Intel was in some manner endorsing the contents of the book. As a result of these various expressed concerns, I was asked to step back from some of the more public roles I had taken as a Christian and not to personally participate in the public launch of my book in China. Reluctantly, and most uncomfortably, I complied with Intel's request. I had been tested in the area of how to properly integrate my faith with my work, and I had failed the test. I had made some minor errors in judgment along the way and was unprepared for the test and challenge that came my way.

Since the publishing of the book, I have been frequently asked about different aspects of the question of integrating your faith with your work. I've often said jokingly that if I were ever asked to write another book, this would be the singular and focused topic. I guess, as a second edition, I now have a chance to give it at least a chapter of attention here and now.

Before the end of this chapter I hope to have challenged you to be an integrated person, one who is the same in the home, in the marketplace, in your hobbies, with your friends, and in the workplace. One who both integrates his or her faith into every aspect of his or her life and demonstrates judgment and effectiveness in how to do so.

ETHICS IN THE WORKPLACE

I've been blessed to work for a company that has worked hard to have and keep a great reputation as an ethical company. Many, however, are not so fortunate. Further, there could be just a few unethical individuals in high places and hundreds or thousands of employees and families influenced in the process. In recent current events, we've seen some of the greatest business tragedies in history.

> After a series of revelations involving irregular accounting procedures bordering on fraud perpetrated throughout the 1990s involving Enron and its accounting firm Arthur Andersen, Enron stood on the verge of undergoing the largest bankruptcy in history by mid-November 2001. Daniel Scotto, an influential financial analyst, stated in August 2001 that Enron was likely to implode, and recommended selling all Enron securities, including common stock. He was also the first to divulge publicly the magnitude of Enron's financial leverage and lack of corporate ethics, and to question the reliability of Enron's reported earnings results, despite those results being audited by Arthur Andersen.[7]

Enron had risen rapidly with aggressive deal making by leveraging use of its assets, which reached claimed revenues of $111 billion in 2000. It was named by *Fortune* magazine as the most innovative company from 1996 to 2001. However, its aggressiveness turned to greed as the company resorted to ever more aggressive techniques to continue its torrid growth. At some point along the way, these techniques moved from aggressive to illegal.

The collapse of Enron was an enormous signal that defined a new era in business much like the breakup of Ma Bell or Standard Oil or the market collapse of 1929. Enron ushered in an entirely new era in the awareness of ethics in business, the repercussions of which continue to be felt in corporate boards and company governance models even to this day. Quickly following Enron were Global Crossing, WorldCom, and now numerous companies admitting to stock-option backdating. Taken together, these events have been like a series of shotgun blasts aimed at the business world in rapid succession. CEO pay is seen as evil and out of control. Corporate executives once seen as leaders to be admired are now vilified as unethical robbers. No longer are they hardworking captains of industry to be followed and honored. Sarbanes-Oxley is now the calling card for corporate regulators with ever more difficult requirements likely to emerge in the future. Corporations across the world today need to raise the bar on ethical leadership. As Christians, we have a tremendous opportunity to be part of the solution to this earnest need.

· · · · ·

On a trip to India once, I had a fabulous speaking engagement to several hundred people. After my speaking time, we opened for questions, and I was deluged with inquires on a wide range of family and business topics. It had been a fabulous evening, and the audience was alive with interest and questions. However, from all the questions, the topic of business ethics was the dominant theme. Many of the questions were detailed and specific in terms of how to handle this matter among peers, with respect to the boss, company business practices, and the like. Many companies in India, Intel included, were finding themselves confronted with such issues, as the Internet economy was soaring, foreign national firms were rapidly placing roots, competition for skilled labor was high, wages were appreciating quickly, and arcane and complex tax laws and traditional business practices were having a hard time keeping up with the changes creating numerous opportunities for misunderstanding, error, and greed.

Against such a backdrop, the question of business ethics couldn't be more relevant or important.

As I've clearly emphasized throughout the book, you must be a great employee. Based on that reputation, you have established the credibility you need to fully exercise your position in the workplace. However, having done that, how far do you go? When you see things that make you uncomfortable, what should you do? Is it part of your job to be a policeman for ethics in the workplace? Do you become seen as an ethical whistle-blower or simply a pain in the sides of management at your company? Is it part of your job as a Christian in the workplace to assure ethics are practiced?

A few guidelines that might be helpful include ...

1. For a simple starting point, make sure you personally are great in this area of business-place ethics. Live above reproach (Titus 3:1–2). Make sure you know the business processes and ethics training your company offers, and make certain you are current on that training.

2. Next, realize you were not hired to run around the company and be the self-appointed ethics officer. Unless you are a member of the audit committee for the company, ensuring business ethics are practiced simply isn't your job or part of your job definition. In any company, particularly larger ones, there are always rumors. It isn't your job to chase them down or to escalate them. Get back to work and ignore the gossip and rumors.

However, you might be in a situation where in the course of your work you are faced with what appears to be questionable business practices. You haven't gone looking for these issues but, lo and behold, there they are confronting you. At this point, your responsibilities as an employee and a Christian become considerable. You now need to take some uncomfortable steps to make sure these practices are appropriately considered. Depending on your corporate structure, this will probably require you to take the situation to your supervisor, financial controller, or audit-committee representative. Of course, given your good training on the matter, you should be able to clearly describe what the violation is that concerns you. Further, you should approach it with clear and solid documentation as to what the issue is. Finally, prepare your comments carefully and thoughtfully before showing up for the meeting with the appropriate individual. This isn't about your feelings; it's about the factual issues you see with the specific situation versus your corporate business-practice policies and possibly those of the appropriate government agency. However, once you have taken this most difficult step, it's important that you let the appropriate individuals handle the investigation and the appropriate follow-through. Having done your job, get back to work.

It's been great to be fortunate enough to be part of a company who views business ethics as essential. While, unfortunately, I've been part of various investigations and lawsuits, Intel's practices are consistently positive and well regarded across the industry and the globe.

However, you may not be as fortunate as I have been. You may be working at a company that follows a path closer to that of Enron—a company that finds the edge of the law and then pushes beyond that edge on a consistent basis. If so, you may need to find a different place of employment. Working in a situation where your conscience is constantly pricked and challenged by the business practices around you is most likely not sustainable for you as an employee.

Over the years, I've counseled a couple of individuals to follow this path, as difficult as that might be. I was pretty stunned by one man who cited issue after issue in the workplace. While by all appearances he was doing the right things by documenting the situations and raising them to his superiors, it appeared the situation wasn't going to be easily rectified. A new place of employment was probably the best route for him to follow.

FULL-TIME MINISTER?

When I speak publicly, I will often ask the audience, "If you are a full-time minister, please raise your hand." Normally I see only a small number of hands raised. Usually there are a few ministers in the audience who feel proud to raise their hands. I often call them out specifically and often ask for a round of applause. Like Isaiah was willing to heed the call, so they have been willing to be full time in their commitment to Christian service.

> Then I heard the voice of the Lord saying, "Whom shall I send? And who will go for us?" And I said, "Here am I. Send me!" (Isa. 6:8)

We should honor our ministers. They have been willing to step forward; they have been willing to commit their lives and full-time professions to the presentation of the gospel.

Often there are a few who sense where I'm going when I ask

the "full-time minister" question. I'll then read Colossians 3:23–24 and ask the question again. More hands rise. I'll then read it again and exhort them that if they are Christians, they have committed themselves to be 100 percent, full-time Christians in everything they do. They cannot compartmentalize their faith into tidy segments of their lives: At work I'm Joe the executive; at home I'm Joe the dad or husband; and at church I'm Joe the Christian.

No, indeed we see that Jesus did the vast majority of his ministry while on the way: on the road, in the market, at the fishing dock, at the wedding, on the hillside, while in the house, or at the well. We certainly see him in the synagogue and at the temple ministering. But it's almost like these occasions seem to be more of a natural outgrowth of his ministering all the time rather than a place he needed to go to minister. We certainly see Paul using the synagogues for ministry as he traveled from place to place, but it was a good starting point for him to begin in a new community, since he knew there would be a gathering of those interested in spiritual matters (Acts 17:2). Today, where can you go to start your ministry? Church is the place where the believers are already gathered. There isn't a synagogue of unreached people gathered and waiting for you to show up with the message.

As we look at the Great Commission, we have that famous passage admonishing us to "go." Many a missionary has used this as a "life verse" of why they chose to head to a far-off mission field.

> Then Jesus came to them and said, "All authority in heaven and on earth has been given to me. Therefore go and make disciples of all nations, baptizing them in the name of the Father and of the Son

and of the Holy Spirit, and teaching them to obey everything I have commanded you. And surely I am with you always, to the very end of the age." (Matt 28:18–20)

However, many scholars now look at this passage and interpret it not so much as a directive "to go" but rather a statement of "as you go." In other words, while you are going, make disciples, baptize them, and teach them.

Thus, we are all full-time ministers. Today, there is a bit of a workplace ministry movement afoot. A number of individuals and writers have risen up on this topic. I consider myself a member and participant in this movement. Some friends of mine are starting businesses in foreign countries with the explicit goal of using those businesses as environments where they can minister and present the gospel to their workforces. Writers such as Os Hilman, Bob Buford, Dennis Bakke, John Beckett, Michael Novak, Wes Cantrell, Rich Marshall, and David Miller have all published recent works on various aspects of faith in the workplace. Knowing many of them and reading their works, I'd certainly recommend reading their books as you continue your journey in this area.

If you call yourself a Christian and claim the name of Jesus as your Lord, you are a full-time minister. You need to be 100 percent his in every situation and circumstance. Isn't it marvelous that Intel, Nike, Boeing, GE, TI, IBM, or whoever your employer is pays your salary and gives you benefits as you go about your daily ministry? But as I've said numerous times, while in the workplace you are first and foremost to be a great employee. However, there are numerous opportunities to present Christ *while* you are being a great employee.

There are an awful lot of minutes squeezed between your formal duties and your informal opportunities.

As we discussed in chapter 7, you are to be a clear and public witness. You are called to be a full-time minister for Christ. Now the question is how to do it: Under what circumstances can you share your faith in the workplace and under what situations should you refrain?

I have two simple guidelines that I've used over the years that have served me pretty well:

Rule #1 — Be yourself, all the time.

Be an integrated, sold-out, and 100 percent Christian all the time and don't be afraid to let that shine through while you are in the workplace or marketplace of life.

After being a Christian for a number of years, I've gained a bit of Christian jargon in my language that I'm not afraid to show in my daily conversation. If you say "Praise the Lord" or such when something wonderful happens, don't be afraid to use the same language when you are in the workplace.

And don't hesitate to be seen as a Christian. Intel has a jet that flies between our campuses. Think of this not like some fancy or elegant executive jet. It is more like a flying bus that could have a newly hired factory worker squeezed into the seat next to the company's CEO. I always take an aisle seat and always do my devotions while flying. I'll get my Bible out and read while the plane is taking off. I have no hesitation in letting people see what I'm doing. It's part of my character, and having a morning devotion is part of me. Recently, one individual, John, noticed this and used the opportunity to get acquainted. He's now visiting our church with his family. Don't hide your faith; be proud of it.

Rule #2—If someone goes to the personal level, you can too!

I've often felt the need for someone to know Christ and hear the gospel. If you sense that urge in different situations, that's wonderful; you're being sensitive to the call of the Holy Spirit. However, when is it appropriate and when is it not?

This simple rule has served me well over the years. If someone engages in the conversation about family, kids, sick relatives or parents, or other personal activities like sports or hobbies, they've opened the door to a personal dialogue with you. They've moved from the professional to the personal level. It's important to note that the other person has done this, not you. It doesn't count if it's you who has chosen to dialogue at the personal level; it's the other person who needs to open the door in the work setting to the personal level of his or her life. Once the door to their personal life has been opened, consider that an opportunity to share at the personal level about your life and about your faith.

I had an administrative assistant for many years who knew well of my faith. She handled many calls and scheduled around my various commitments and speaking engagements. However, she always kept a clear separation of her personal matters from professional ones and never raised in conversation or questioned my faith. To her, my workplace witness was simply that: whatever she saw in my lifestyle as demonstrating Christ.

In contrast to that example, I was recently approached by my

Intel coworker Matthew, who asked about a potential mentoring relationship. Mentoring in the workplace is encouraged at Intel and, thus, I often get such inquiries. Further, given my book and speaking on the subject, I often get such requests on a personal level as well. With many such inquires I tend to be quite selective and usually have an informal interview with the individual to judge their seriousness and my ability to provide some assistance to them before agreeing to any form of sustained mentoring relationship with them.

Matthew and I arranged dinner when we both happened to be traveling to the same location. He worked in my group, but I didn't really know much about him. He seemed smart enough, had a good reputation, and was anxious to be even more successful and have a broader impact in the company than he already had. Very early in the dinner it became quite clear that Matthew was familiar with the first edition of this book. Also, he was open and desirous of a relationship at not only the professional level, but at the personal level as well. With the door open, so to speak, I was free to walk in and share knowledge from my work, my family, and my faith. In a short amount of time, Matthew, his wife, and his children began visiting with us at church. I was able to talk about my faith in great detail with him. Linda and I were able to respond to questions and concerns that he and his wife had. We got to know his kids and began to share our family with theirs. In not too many months, Matthew took advantage of our hot tub and was baptized into Christ on Easter Sunday. Today, he and his family are thriving in their newfound Christian family, regularly sharing seats next to us at church and in other functions.

As Matthew has reflected on our first discussions since then, in good humor he says he opened the door a crack and I busted it off its hinges. More seriously, when the door is opened by the other, feel free to walk in and begin sharing your life and passions. If the other person is uncomfortable, you will quickly find out. If they are uncomfortable, you need to immediately honor their anxiety and back off. However, if it's a divine appointment, you would be ignoring the Spirit's call not to take every opportunity to use that opportunity for Christ. Go for it.

INTEGRITY IN EVERYTHING

Since the fall of man, we all make mistakes. It's called sin. Almost every leader in the Bible is recorded with not just their successes, but also their failings. From Abraham to Moses to David to Paul to Peter—in black and white for everyone down the centuries to read— you find the errors of the great Bible leaders recorded in eternity. This is one of the things that testifies to me that the Bible is the valid Word of God—its audacious and sometimes raw and brutal honesty. If I were writing a book to define a religion that millions would follow, would I write the failings of all my leaders in great detail? Not likely!

As you walk through life balancing the demands of work, family, and faith, one of the most important elements is your reputation and character. Are you living a life of impeccable purity (Phil. 4:8)? Are you living a life above reproach? Do you guard your eyes, your heart, and your mind from the temptations of this world?

I travel a lot and spend many evenings alone in hotel rooms. After a long day it's pretty easy to flip on the TV and channel surf.

Not everything you'll find on hotel TV channels is appropriate for Christian eyes to watch. While Linda and I have a policy not to watch R-rated movies, when you are a thousand miles from home, who would know if you watched that flick that enticed you but unfortunately violated the standards you might have set for yourself and your family? I've set a personal policy to simply leave the TV off while traveling. I have my PC loaded up with a collection of Christian MP3s. I turn them on and use the time wisely—I can almost always use some hours to catch up on work!

I also make myself very available to Linda. Cell phones are wonderful things. She can call me just about any time and has certainty that she can inquire what I'm doing, day or night. Of course, such availability has had a few interesting moments like when I'm onstage giving a speech, having forgotten to turn my cell phone off. "Hi, darling. Hundreds of people are now watching me talk with you right now." With time-zone changes, she might get a dreary, hoarse, and somber "Yes, dear…." Of course, sometimes I just can't take her call at that moment due to a meeting or speech or whatever. I make every attempt to step out and call her back as quickly as possible. This absolute availability is just another opportunity to bolster her confidence and help hold me accountable to a life of integrity.

On international trips I often find many people know me whom I don't know. Given my visible role at Intel, many people are interested to meet me, and I usually try to make myself rather accessible. On one trip I greeted a woman who seemed to be trying hard to get my attention. Her English skills were very poor. Through a broken conversation and uneasiness in my spirit, I became convinced that it wasn't an appropriate situation. I quickly removed myself from the situation, uncertain of what she might have been pursuing, but certain it was best not to find out.

The Internet makes information accessible everywhere, both good and bad. You are just one click away from great sites and similarly one click away from smut and porn. I had one individual ask me recently if I could have Intel IT monitor the sites he visits to help keep him more accountable. I admired his zeal for purity. Likewise, while I enjoy having a MySpace account to check out my kids' MySpace sites, the "friend requests" are sometimes far from appropriate. You don't need to click on every link to find where it leads. Look at the source of the link and you can almost always tell if it's taking you to some place you have no business seeing.

At Intel, executives will typically have a technical assistant. On one occasion I had a female assistant who was traveling with me. She was having some computer difficulties, and being a geek, I felt capable to assist her. I went to her room to help get her network connection running properly. After the door closed to her room, I realized what a stupid situation I had placed myself in. I sought forgiveness from Linda for my indiscretion immediately thereafter.

As Linda and I approach empty nesting, it's becoming easier to have Linda join me on business trips, which is great. I look forward to helping my balance by being able to mix a few days of pleasure with an obligatory business trip. However, this will make it even easier to blur the lines between work and personal items. (Did I really need to make that trip?) It will also make it easy to blur the lines on what is an Intel versus a personal item on my expense report.

Similarly, as my administrative assistant handles so many of my calendar items, it's pretty easy to blur the line and ask her to do a personal item or two for me. It's even easy to rationalize: If I had to take time out of my normal workday to do this, it would be taking away time I would be spending on Intel business. Thus, asking her to do some personal items would be making me even more productive. Of course, all these are situations where we as Christians need to be role models, absolutely squeaky clean and avoiding even the appearance of questionable behavior.

HOW DO YOU LIVE A LIFE
OF ABSOLUTE INTEGRITY?

1. Avoid compromising situations.

Simply put, don't place yourself in compromising situations like I did with my assistant in the hotel room. If you feel a discomfort in your spirit, treat that like an alarm bell and get out of there quickly.

One time when I was just a young boy of ten years or so, our family minister asked me on my way out of church on Sunday how I was doing. I said that I was not so well because I had fallen out of bed the night before. He asked why I thought I fell out of bed, to which I replied, "I guess I stayed too close to where I got into it!" The next Sunday that was the subject of his sermon: how we as Christians should not be staying too close to where we entered into our faith. Instead of staying close to areas of temptation or challenge, areas where we just want to have our curiosity tickled, we need to avoid them entirely. This is a wonderful yet sometimes challenging aspect about Linda: She doesn't see the world in grays but in pure black and white. While I might be able to rationalize a topic, she can very quickly determine where the line is and declare it good or bad.

2. Be accountable.

Use your mentor or accountability partner or spouse to openly share your areas of weakness. Ask them to inquire of you in these areas, and commit to being honest and transparent with them in return. Ask others to surround you in prayer in those areas, like a hedge of protection (Job 1:10). Make yourself available to your spouse 24/7 when you are traveling. Commit to them that they can reach you any time and have freedom to inquire what you are doing.

3. When in doubt, don't.

If you aren't sure, don't even get close to it. The few dollars you might save or the benefit you may receive just isn't worth the risk of compromising your integrity. It would be most easy to claim a few things on expense reports that would seem perfectly okay: *Hmm, I need to access the Internet when I'm on a cruise ship vacationing with Linda as I work on the book. Of course, I'll check my work e-mail so it really is a business expense, now isn't it?* All of these are little opportunities to cross the line into gray. Don't do it.

4. Fill yourself with the Word of God and then apply it.

The best way to live a life of absolute integrity is to apply God's Word directly and specifically to those situations as they arise. Seek godly characteristics as defined in Galatians 5:22–23. Grow up the ladder of Christian maturity as seen in 2 Peter 1:5–11. If you struggle with lust, memorize a passage like Job 31:1 and recite it whenever you might be tempted. If you struggle with gossip, read Ephesians 4:25 or 5:19. If you have ill thoughts toward a coworker, spend time on Matthew 5:22. These are just a few examples that might be helpful. The key is, whatever circumstance you are challenged with personally, choose a passage or two, memorize it, and claim it regularly to help battle those areas in which you struggle.

WHAT YOU DO VERSUS WHAT YOU BELIEVE

I love my job. The first time I touched a computer, I knew that was what I wanted to do with the rest of my life. While I certainly have had bad days and particular assignments that I just didn't enjoy, I generally have great enthusiasm for the role that I am in. If you've ever heard me speak publicly about technology, my enthusiasm and passion will certainly come through. I just love it!

When I speak in internal settings at Intel, I will often encourage people to find a job they enjoy. Sometimes I'll even be a bit challenging and tell them if they don't have passion for what they are doing, it is best for them and their team if they would move on to something else and allow someone else with passion to fill that position.

When I speak on behalf of Intel, I will often describe my vision: that there would be a bit of Intel technology that is touching every human on the planet, in every aspect of their lives—work, learn, play—every minute of every day.

When I speak as a Christian, I describe my vision: that there would be a bit of Intel technology that is touching every human on the planet, in every aspect of their lives—work, learn, play—every minute of every day so that many more might hear the gospel of Christ.

As you can quickly notice, the two are in harmony with each other. I can see how the things that I do daily are creating more capabilities for people to have computers, communications devices, access to the Internet, and the infrastructure to provide those services. I know that while these technologies have utilitarian purposes (as well as some unfortunate evil side effects such as pornography), they are also being used to reach the world for Christ.

Since the Pax Romana of the Roman Empire, the human population has not been as connected as it will be by the Internet in the next decade or so. Somehow I think that the time of Christ's arrival was specifically ordained by God knowing that the world was "most connected" to hear the message of Christ. I have this idea in the back of my mind that maybe, just maybe, that the second coming will be ushered forward when the world is again "the most connected." Thus, I feel that maybe every time we make another chip, we just might be hastening the day of his coming. With that in mind, I actively engage with a number of ministries that make aggressive use of the Internet to reach the world with the gospel message. Synergies such as this further reinforce my passion for what I do in my assignment at Intel: Connect the world using Intel technology.

I'm a great believer in the potential for technology. Gordon Moore, one of Intel's founders, made an observation that the transistors on a chip double every two years. You can imagine that when he made this observation and chips had a few hundred transistors, he couldn't have imagined forty years later we'd be building chips with over a billion transistors on them! Not only has the observation been a true guidepost for the industry for forty years, it will continue to be for many years to come as well. Semiconductor circuits that we build will continue to become more and more powerful microprocessors. These microprocessors will enable us to make computers smaller and more mobile. We'll be able to build computers larger and more powerful. We will be able to solve problems that we've never been able to solve before. We will cure incurable diseases. We will find new sources for energy. We will improve the quality of lives for humans across the planet as a result. It's because of these kinds of confident certainties that I show up for work each day both passionate and optimistic about what I do at work. I believe these efforts will have both earthly and eternal benefits.

I once heard a story about an insurance agent who was passionate that his purpose in selling life insurance was to give families lifetime security. He wasn't selling insurance policies; he was ensuring financial health even if physical health wasn't the case. As the story went, he became aware that Martin Luther King did not have life insurance. He purposed to seek him out. Eventually, he was able to meet with him and secure him a life-insurance policy. As you can imagine, his family greatly benefited from that salesman's passionate view of his bigger assignment. This simple story further emphasizes what I already believed, that we can't view our work as a compartment where the work personality shows up. No, as stated at the beginning of this chapter, we each need to strive to be an integrated person where the personality that shows up at faith, family, work, and play is in fact one in the same. When people meet you in any of these capacities, they've met the same person that is in all the other roles as well. God's call is that we are integrated and effectual witnesses for him in all that we do.

If you despise your work, your witness will undoubtedly be weakened. If you see your job as painful monotony performed out of sheer financial necessity or obligation, you need to consider changing one of two things: your attitude or your job. I don't have a Pollyanna view of work. Since the fall of man in Genesis 3:17–19 we see that man is cursed to toil or labor. Work will not all be fun, and there will be many occasions where you do it out of obligation and commitment. There will be periods when you are just "doing the job" to get somewhere else. I worked on my uncle's farms, a neighbor's horse farm, a radio and TV station, and even a short stint of twenty-six minutes at McDonald's! Maybe a job in college is nothing more than earning some funds for the next year's tuition. Maybe there simply isn't any other possible position available right now that allows you to work and to provide. We will certainly be faced with those situations. However, as we studied in chapter 5, you still need to be a great employee. As we saw in Colossians 3:23–24, you work for the Lord Jesus Christ!

EMBRACING FAILURE

A number of years ago I had an assignment to start up a new business area for Intel in video conferencing. The project was personally godfathered by none other than Andy Grove. It was a huge assignment for me: launching a new business for Intel, starting a new category of products for our customers, and creating a new technology spiral for the industry. It required in-depth engagement with the communications companies and technologies, an area where both Intel and I were quite naive. In many ways, I was simply not prepared for such a daunting assignment. It wasn't clear if any of the new ideas could succeed, but I was certainly determined to try.

For a while it looked like we were going to be successful, indeed. We made some big deals with the service providers and were starting to get some traction. However, after several years, the category was still nascent and product sales were slow. As failure looked more likely, I responded by working even harder and being even more aggressive. I had succeeded in most everything I had done for Intel up to this point and I wasn't about to let this become a blemish on my record. The more likely failure appeared, the harder I worked. I was desperate for continued success.

Finally, after almost four years of effort, I was fired from this assignment. I couldn't believe it. I went home at midday—something unheard of for me. I was distraught and defeated.

This being one of the most visible and significant failures of my career, I had much soul-searching to do. Slowly, I unraveled the key lessons from multiple perspectives. What were the technical and business aspects of the failure? What were the organizational lessons? What were the personal lessons? In this and a number of other situations I've come to realize that failure is where real learning occurs. When you are successful, you are so proud and happy that you overlook the numerous areas in which you could have done even better. Only when you fail do you have the motivation to do the deep soul-searching needed to really learn and grow. We see over and over in Scripture that God uses failure to bring his leaders to that next level of maturity. Imagine Peter's heartbreak after his denial of Christ and Christ's questioning of him after the resurrection. Would you expect Peter to be the vocal leader on Pentecost, the rock of the church? However, after a jarring failure,

Peter makes a great comeback, grows mightily, and just a few days later is giving the sermon of a lifetime (Acts 2).

As humans, when we fail, we are often ready to quickly sweep it under the carpet or stick it in the closet. Instead, these are the great opportunities we have for growth. As this section is titled, embrace failure, search your soul, pray in earnest, and use these situations as impetus to grow. While they may be unpleasant, embrace these situations and consider them deeply. These are the experiences that will truly bring you to the point of integrating your faith with your family and with your work.

· · · · ·

We began this chapter with the challenge to be an integrated person. When someone who might know you at your place of worship sees you in the workplace or at the ball game or at the gym, does he see the same person? Psychologists refer to people who behave radically differently at different times as having multiple personality disorder. Often they are considered schizophrenic: emotionally unstable or detached from reality. This is an extreme mental disorder. However, imagine if someone were watching you in the various settings of your life. Would they see the same person throughout the day or someone who appears to have multiple personalities? Of course, someone does see you throughout the day and in every situation you find yourself. When God looks at you, does he see spiritual schizophrenia? He wants to declare to you someday soon, "Well done, my good and faithful servant. You've been faithful in every role I found you."

· · · · ·

CHAPTER 8 QUESTIONS

1. Do you have ethics situations in the workplace that you feel like you need to address?

2. Do you consider yourself a "full-time minister" in the workplace? Why or why not?

3. What are some simple rules for circumstances where you would or wouldn't share your faith in the workplace?

4. What are some practical steps for how you would be able to be a Christian witness in the workplace?

5. In what areas do you see your integrity being challenged? What are some practical steps to avoid those challenges? What are some Scriptures that might address those challenges?

6. What are some practical suggestions for being a witness through your job?

7. Are you an integrated person when you show up for work? The same person that you are in your home and place of worship? If not, what steps can you take to start bringing yourself into harmony?

9

· · · · ·

Power Juggling

· · · · ·

AFTER READING TO THIS point, you might be tempted to think I've got it all together as a juggler of life's demands. Wrong! I didn't write this book because I'm perfect. Rather, writing it has reminded me of how much work I still have to do to juggle my duties and priorities properly.

As Linda's and my score sheet remind me, I'm working and traveling too much these days. Time for God and time for family are again in short supply. I don't need your admiration; I need your prayers. Like the apostle Paul in Philippians 3:14, I want to press on toward the prize God offers for faithfulness to his calling. And like you, I find that a constant struggle.

God is still teaching me, and I'm still learning. I hope that's true of you as well.

The chapters of this book have been presented in what I believe is the right order for working through them in your life.

SET A COURSE

Personal mission: Begin by establishing a game plan for what you want your values to be: your personal mission statement. Decide what you want to accomplish in your life, and start setting a course that gets you there. We have so little of this precious resource called time, and once you have spent it, you cannot get any of it back. Use it only in a manner consistent with your values and goals.

YOUR HIGHEST VALUE

Prioritize God: Create a unique relationship between yourself and God that is consistently reinforced by your use of time. Create patterns and reminders in your life to help you remain in consistent dialogue and relationship with him. Be a visible and committed member of your place of worship. Use all your resources and finances consistent with God as your first priority.

FIRMLY ESTABLISH YOUR SECOND-HIGHEST VALUE

Prioritize family: Establish your schedule so that other things do not squeeze out precious family time. Date your spouse. Spend individual time with each of your children. Put clear boundaries in place between work and family time. Be flexible, but when a season of work becomes prominent, make sure to take a period of focused time with your family to restore that proper balance.

HAVE BOTH GOD AND WORK IN PROPER ORDER

Work hard: Be a great employee. Realize that ultimately you are not working for your boss, your president, or your company. Instead, you are working for God. In the end, his "Well done" is the only reward that really matters. With the goal of heaven in view, look past anything that might distract you from being a great employee.

KEEP TRUE TO YOUR MISSION STATEMENT

Develop a set of mentors: Create a network of individuals who keep you on track. Find one or two people you trust and respect, and who are good in the areas that you are weak to be mentors to your personal and professional life. Look for both peers to keep you accountable and mentees who could benefit from your experience.

HAVE A CLEAR WITNESS

Having developed a balanced life, with God, family, and work as your priorities, you will also develop a reputation as a great employee. That is when you are in position to be a clear witness for God at your job. You will have developed the credibility to influence others.

INTEGRATE FAITH INTO
YOUR WORK AND FAMILY

This is the graduate-level course in the area of balance. Given the work on balance, you can begin to fully realize your true character in the workplace. You will learn how to be an effective witness in whatever workplace situation you are in. Your sense of ethical situations and how to handle them becomes more acute. Finally, you will be well situated to embrace failures and challenges in life as you never have before.

Returning to the image of a juggler: You're still trying to spin a saucer in the air for God, a salad plate for work, and a serving platter for your family (with teens). These seven principles haven't changed the number or size of the plates or how fast you need to spin them to keep them from falling. However, I hope they've given you some skills that can be applied consistently to the juggling task. Perhaps now you can begin to drop them less often, decrease the size of a few, and consciously decide when and if you should add another plate consistent with your long-term mission.

Applying these principles day in and day out is not easy. As I mentioned before, this is a journey. I'm still learning much in the process myself. I still fail in living by these priorities, and while I offer my personal mission statement as a model for your own, I have a long way to go in accomplishing my goals.

Life today moves at an incredible speed. Don't be so foolish as to believe that after the next project or after the next assignment or when summer comes, you'll somehow get your family back on track and so on. I've heard it said that one definition of insanity is doing the same thing over and over and expecting different results. Things will not miraculously improve. You need to make some conscious decisions and trade-offs.

My prayer and desire for you is that some of the principles and examples in this book will help you to master your priorities and make the right trade-offs. May God's love and mercy surround you and his Holy Spirit fill you as you progress in your journey. Tomorrow, when you arise to begin your day of juggling, may you be purpose-filled and deliberate in your desires, decisions, and directions. To waste time is a great evil; to use it wisely is the greatest blessing of a master juggler.

Afterword

Insights from a Juggler's Wife

by *Linda Gelsinger*

. . . . .

By now, you have a pretty clear view of what kind of person Pat is: a type-A, on-the-go, anxious-to-run-do-and-see type of person. Sometimes I tire just by listening to him describe his day, much less trying to keep up with him! In contrast, I much more enjoy a quiet day at home, doing some chores, going to the gym to work out, spending some time reading a book, and maybe doing a few of my many hobbies. Living with someone like Pat is certainly a wild adventure! And it's divine that our lifestyles and personalities balance each other.

I have had the privilege of attending some of Pat's speaking engagements where he speaks about this book. I love sitting in the audience, reliving the stories and experiences that we have had over our twenty-five years of marriage, and reflecting on how God has grown us and changed us to be more like him. After the event, when it is time to greet those who have come, several have asked me, "When are you going to write your book?" I would laugh with them about such a humorous question. But, sincerely, they wanted to know, from my perspective, how to live with a man like Pat who loves the Lord and is also very driven and passionate in all that he does. Well, writing a book is beyond what I have ever thought of doing, but when asked if I would write an afterword to conclude this book, with some apprehension I agreed. I hope this view from the other side may help to show how I support, encourage, and love my husband.

Let me tell you a bit about myself so you can have a more thorough understanding of my relationship with Pat. I grew up learning about the Lord at a very early age. My first recollection about church was walking to Sunday school with my older brother, Rick. I clearly remember my fourth-grade Sunday school teacher and how she loved me. And I vividly recall how she always hugged me and made me feel like I was the most special person in the room. Her acceptance of me went a long way toward my accepting the Lord and being baptized at eleven years of age. I continued to make church a priority in my life as I was growing up, and attended because I wanted to learn more about Jesus and how to be like him.

When I reached my high school years, many of my girlfriends had boyfriends. I was quiet, shy, and really didn't talk to boys at all. This became a problem for me, because I wanted a boyfriend like my friends did. I remember walking home from school very discouraged one day. I prayed about it and sensed that God told me to simply wait on him for the right person. I had just a handful of dates in high school and was determined to wait for God's timing. I met Pat when I was twenty-one years old, and the rest is history! And it was definitely worth the wait!

As you read in chapter 1, when Pat and I were dating he was very goal oriented. He had his ten-year plan down, complete with goals for his job and career as well as his scholastic goals. My aspiration was to obtain some education, find a job that would support me—but most of all I wanted to be married, have children, and be a full-time mother. When Pat asked me what my goals were, I was very hesitant to tell him. Could I really tell a guy I was just beginning to date that my greatest desire was to get married and have children? Luckily, yes—and now I've invested almost twenty-five years of my time, energy, and love into the kids. I am proud of them and continue to be excited about how God is directing their lives.

FILLING THE VOID

We are now on the verge of being empty nesters. Elizabeth is living on her own, Josiah and Nathan are in college, and Micah is a senior in high school. While the children's absence has a modest impact on Pat, it presents an enormous change for me and my daily life. I didn't ask to retire from motherhood. And, frankly, I am not ready to be done with it! I love being a mom. While some may desire a career beyond being a mother, I want to spend as much time as I can being the best mother God made me to be for my children.

Thus a challenge at this point of my life is dealing with the loneliness that has come with Pat being gone often for work. The kids no longer fill the house with noise and joy, nor does it take every second of my day and night to keep up with them. So I have been working on how not just to fill that time with stuff, but to find where God wants me to be at this point in my life. I co-led women's ministries at church and was involved in leading a mentoring program. Now

I have started pursuing a hands-on ministry outside of the church walls where I can continue to use my passion for mentoring.

I also have hobbies that I very much enjoy. In fact, we have just finished a remodel at our house that has given me a very large craft room. I really enjoy scrapbooking, card making, and quilting. I try to balance my time with these crafts, using the skills that I have to bless our family and others. One of my most recent projects is to make baby quilts for needy mommas and their babies. I pray over the material as I sew, so that when the baby gets the quilt, it is bathed in prayer.

Besides volunteering and crafting, I now am finding more time to travel with Pat. He has always desired that I accompany him on business travel, but until recently, it hasn't been possible because of my motherly responsibilities to the children. With Micah graduating and going off to college in the fall, travel with Pat will be possible. Of course, I will be choosy about which travel I will do with him. I've definitely decided to avoid the crazy two-week trips where he is in a different country or hotel almost every night!

Pat also desires that I become more involved in the speaking opportunities about balancing faith, family, and work. I have attended a few events with him over the last couple of years but plan to become more visible in the future. Now when I say that, I don't mean more visible onstage, just being more visible in the front row of the audience! Pat is the one who likes speaking in public—not me! By traveling with him to speaking engagements, I'll be able to meet, connect, and encourage women who attend.

Having had the privilege of being a stay-at-home wife and mom, in the early years of our marriage I felt very uncomfortable going to the business dinners and meeting all the professional wives of Pat's coworkers. When I expressed this to him, he graciously started introducing me as, "This is my wife, Linda. She has the most important job in the world, and that is staying at home caring for our children." This gave me importance, purpose, and encouragement! Most of the wives were moms too, so it gave us some common topics of discussion. In addition, many of them were also stay-at-home moms, and they appreciated Pat introducing me in this validating way.

Over the years, I have even found attending business events to be fun. We usually travel there and back together, get to stay in a beautiful hotel room, and enjoy a wonderful meal together. Even though we share the mealtime with hundreds of others, it gives me an opportunity to meet some of Pat's coworkers and gives me a little more understanding of his role in the business world. Besides, I'm proud of him!

As you've learned, Pat travels a lot. It is not unusual for him to be gone four out of five days a week. One way that Pat really helps me survive is that he is almost always available via phone. Often that means I pull him out of a meeting, but since I usually have a purpose and don't call just to chat, he can talk to me for a minute, address the questions, and then get back to work. I don't abuse that either. Knowing that he is busy and that I am pulling him away, I choose when to interrupt him and when to wait. E-mail is a great way to communicate less urgent issues with him. But still, he usually responds quickly to that as well.

Volunteering, crafting, and traveling are all things that help fill the void with Pat's business-trip schedule. But the bottom line is Pat is frequently traveling. I find that I handle his busyness very well ... part of the time. Sometimes, though, things seem to fall apart and I get upset with him either for being gone or being too busy. I have found that two things help in this area: clear expectations and a proper mind-set.

Have clear expectations.

If I communicate to Pat and ask him his plans, I know what to expect. We have slowly learned over the years how important it is to set clear expectations with each other. I expect that when he walks in the door after work, he is ready to spend the next few hours with me. While that is his plan, there is just one exception—he just has one or two quick things to complete first. If he lets me know this right away, I try to be patient and wait. So simply laying out expectations to each other clears up confusion and protects us both from frustration.

I have learned a very valuable thing about Pat: He is not a mind reader! Pat is like most men and just isn't as sensitive to those emotional cues I might think are so obvious. So, if I sit in the other room, simply hoping that he will stop doing what he is doing and spend time with me, I am setting myself up for defeat. I have found that it is not effective to yell from the other room, "It would be nice for you to spend some time with me!" A better strategy would be to walk into the room, sit on his lap, and ask when he might be done so we can spend some time together.

When Pat started his "at home" chart, it really helped us to take the emotion out of the "You are never home" discussion. I think the most positive thing this chart has done is to encourage Pat to come home when he can so the points are more on the positive side. As a goal-oriented person, he is working toward racking up some points in this area. He arranges his meetings to be early rather than late so he can be home by 5:00 or 6:15. Of course, I'll occasionally catch him in the garage on his cell phone finishing that last call and racing in before the deadline! This chart helps me to see that, yes, he might have had a bad month, but I see him working to make the next month better.

Sometimes Pat is the one to set the expectations, and sometimes I am. It doesn't really matter who takes the initiative—just so one of us does. And, of course, being flexible with those expectations is important, as things do change. Sometimes just the fact that Pat sets them helps me to feel important in his life.

Have a proper mind-set and attitude.

Besides setting clear expectations, a second thing that has helped me handle his being gone is my mind-set. If I know he is going to be busy, I try to plan something that will keep me occupied. If he is out of town for two weeks, I try to plan my schedule to eliminate times when I would be lonely. When he calls home while he is on a trip, having a pleasant, happy wife to talk to is so much better than a complaining, negative one. If I say, "I am really missing you and cannot wait for you to be home," it makes him more anxious to come home to me. It is so much more pleasant and fun to have his arrival home be positive and encouraging, and to be able to spend the time together in joy instead of struggles.

With Pat's busy schedule, I have found that I need to be cautious about getting used to him being gone. I think for me, sometimes it is easier to handle not seeing him if I remove myself from it emotionally.

But, the danger in that is that when he is home, I am not visibly excited about it! I need to balance the emotional part of me not to become overly emotional when he is gone or have an "I don't care" attitude when he is home.

A proper mind-set during discussions is also important. When Pat and I disagree on a problem, I have learned not to get emotional about it. It frustrates him, and then I just get more frustrated. It's sort of a crazy cycle where both of us lose touch with the issue and get distracted by the emotion of the situation. I try very hard to remain logical (which is often hard for me, as it is with a lot of women) and explain my point of view. I also try not to use the words *always* or *never*. While in my emotional state, I really feel like what those two *absolute* words represent is true in this circumstance, although that's rarely the case. As soon as I say something like that, Pat feels defeated, defensive, and his logical mind races to prove me wrong. Thus, we end up discussing why it isn't "always" or "never" and sometimes never get back to the main issue. That said, my goal is to avoid too much emotion and to choose my words carefully.

Being joyful hasn't always been something that has come easy to me. While I am happy most of the time, having an attitude of constant true joyfulness is harder for me. Over the years, I have memorized verses about joyfulness and prayed that God would help me develop this quality. I am still praying about this in fact! It might always appear on my prayer list, but that is okay. It helps to keep it in the front of my mind. Sometimes joyfulness is a choice I make too. My attitude can also help in this area. If my first interaction with Pat is filled with a joyful attitude, chances are that we'll have a very good day with each other.

Submission can be a very negative word in a person's life, especially to some women. Pat is a great husband and leader, and early in our married life, I decided that he would be the head of our household and that I would practice Colossians 3:18, which reads, "Wives, submit to your husbands, as is fitting in the Lord." Pat is open to my suggestions and opinions, but the final decision falls on him. The final responsibility also falls on him, and I know that God will use those opportunities to make Pat the godly man he is supposed to be. And I can support him with a proper mind-set, emotions, and a joyful and submissive attitude.

BEING SUPPORTIVE

Besides altering my schedule, expectations, or mind-set, here are a few practical tips on how I have learned to be more supportive:

1. As things have broken around the house, I have, over the years, learned to fix them. I remember the first time I took the battery off our riding mower and took it in to get it replaced. I felt so capable and self-confident! And Pat was pleasantly surprised (and our lawn was nicely mown too). Instead of another thing adding to his too-busy schedule, I could take care of it for him. If I cannot fix it though (I draw the line at plumbing issues), I have learned to hire it out. I might not know about fixing water heaters, but if it is leaking all over the garage floor, I have learned how to ask questions and make wise decisions about how to take care of it.

2. Take our cars in for repair and inspections.

3. Learn how to mow the lawn. I learned early in my marriage
   that mowing the lawn was great fun, and I enjoy the
   feeling of accomplishment when I'm finished. It also was a
   wonderful break for me as the kids weren't allowed on the
   grass when I was mowing. And it was one less thing Pat
   had to spend time doing on evenings or weekends.

4. Sleep. Pat gets along just fine each day on four to five hours
   of sleep. I, on the other hand, am more normal and need
   seven to eight hours of sleep on a consistent basis. So, I
   have allowed myself to take naps during the days when
   I know he is getting home late or if I know he will be
   returning home late in the evening from a business trip. I
   can happily nap any time, so occasionally it works for me
   to take a short nap in the early evening, and then when Pat
   gets home late in the evening from a trip, I can actually
   stay up till midnight to be with him.

5. Pray. One time Pat made a decision that I totally disagreed
   with. I told him I disagreed with it, and he still made the
   decision. I was so upset with him! Couldn't he see my
   point of view? Didn't he understand that the decision he
   made really hurt me? So I had two choices. Choice one:
   I could continue to be mad at him, and repeatedly bring
   it up to him. Choice two: I could let it go, and simply
   continue to pray about it. Fortunately, this time I made
   the right decision and just kept on praying about it and
   didn't bring it up with him again. After a few months, the
   Lord showed him the decision was not the right one, and

Pat corrected it. Isn't it better when we let the Lord deal with those things and not get in between? Of course, the best and most useful type of support is to pray for Pat. I pray for his health, his travel safety, his success in his business, and his spiritual health, just to name a few.

6. Having fun with the kids. Making the time fun with the kids when Pat was gone was important too. While the normal day-to-day school/sports/music lessons/friends occupied much of our time when the kids were younger, I also tried to make some fun and special family activities that the kids would enjoy.

- Letting one child choose the menu for the night, go shopping with them for the ingredients, and then work together to make it. We might have had some interesting combinations, but they were healthy enough and the kids loved doing it. It was also a great time to teach them about good preparation and nutrition as well. We still talk about the night that all we had for dinner was fruit kabobs … yet we still managed to get our five food groups for the day in.

- French-fry night was fun too, although not very nutritious. I would have the kids get in their pj's, and we would load in the van and drive through McDonald's for some french fries. Another non-nutritious thing we ate were glazed doughnuts on the way to school, or Blizzards from Dairy Queen on the way home.

- Having breakfast for dinner. Pat liked his potato/meat/ veggies for dinner, so he wasn't keen on breakfast at night. But the kids sure loved it! It was sort of a "Dad's gone—let's do breakfast again, okay, Mom?" Instead of missing Dad, they knew there was something special that we did only when he was traveling.

- Making the living room/dining room into a fort area. All we needed were blankets, sheets, and a few pieces of strategically placed furniture, and the kids were amused for hours (and sometimes days.) Even though I like a clean and organized house, I could certainly live with the tent fort for a while if it brought enjoyment for the kids.

- Mom and daughter time! We had a neighborhood teenage boy who would come over to babysit our three boys. The boys loved it as he would romp, roll, and wrestle like Dad would with them. This gave Elizabeth and me the opportunity to slip away to do some shopping or go to a movie and dinner. Making special time with the oldest, and the only daughter, was important. I know she appreciated this time away with me, and I loved it!

- Especially when the children were younger, I tried to make it fun when Pat had been gone a lot and would plan something for us all to look forward to do together when he got home. We would plan dinner out and a movie, or maybe a big breakfast on Saturday morning, complete with homemade hash browns, bacon, coffee cake, pancakes, and scrambled eggs!

- These days, traveling to see our children at college also

occupies my time. Josiah and Nathan especially love it when I come to visit. We usually spend some time at the mall and the grocery store together. Somehow, boys in college still like Mom to shop and cook for them. They probably eat for a month on what we buy. And, it makes this lover-of-shopping momma happy!

· · · · ·

While supporting Pat is very important, I've also found that encouragement remains a big factor as well. I remember a particular time when Pat was very discouraged with a problem at work. While it isn't my "job" to fix his problems, and seldom can I fix them (or even understand them), I can sympathize and try to encourage him. One way I do this is to tuck a note in his Bible. I don't tell him it's there; he just finds it when he is reading. He knows I am thinking about him, praying for him, and will support him regardless of how the crises of the day are resolved.

Sometimes all I need to do is just sit with him, with my arm around him to comfort him, while he tells me about what's discouraging him.

Sometimes it is as simple as spending time with him, even being quiet. Remember, many men like time together that isn't filled with talk; just being together can be helpful.

When our kids were young, I never had to worry about greeting Pat when he first came home from work—we had four kids to do that! And you can be sure that when the boys came to wrestle—I mean, *greet* their dad—I was far away! Partly for protection and partly from being tempted to say, "Someone is going to get hurt."

Now that Micah is the only one home, and he is so often gone at work or out with friends, I have found I need to stop and anticipate when Pat is coming home and get ready to welcome him.

And that doesn't mean greet him with words right away. I may have thousands of words to say as I might have been home all day with no one to talk to, but Pat doesn't want to walk into a house and have me start unloading on him with the many words I have stored up and all the issues of my day. So, I try to hug and kiss him, and start by asking about his day first. Of course, if his mind hasn't quite entirely switched out of Intel mode yet, I might need to make it several good, long kisses!

One of the ways I encourage Pat is to make some of the small decisions. After he spends all day working and making tons of decisions, I have found that it helps him if I decide what we are going to do when he gets home. After dealing with hundreds of employees, products, and customers, he really doesn't want to make yet another decision. In the beginning when he had me make the decisions about where to go or what to eat, it made me feel like he didn't care. But I've realized he's simply "decision-ed" out.

Besides the roles of supporter and encourager, I also take on the responsibility of being a challenger. Pat has always called me his "balance," especially when he is out of control. I try to reign him back in and encourage him to plan less and have a little rest. It doesn't work to get mad at him or accuse him of being a workaholic. We know he works a lot, and he enjoys doing it. Since my goal is often to help slow him down, if I come from a different point of view, it usually helps.

That is one reason we purchased a vacation home. It is a

place where we can get away, relax, slow down a bit, and just be separate from his normal busy days. Of course, it is an added incentive for him to get that marvelous sticky bun at the bakery after a long bike ride. It also helps him to relax if I allow him to do the few e-mails that need to be done so he can get the matter off his mind a little bit.

• • • • •

Being Pat's wife is a job … a full-time job. It has required me to push out of my comfort zone into his work arena and change my lifestyle as our kids have grown. On a day-to-day basis it necessitates communicating clear expectations and having a proper and emotionally controlled mind-set. Supporting Pat practically and encouraging him in small and big ways all contribute to his success. Challenging him with love and understanding is essential for our marriage as well. I don't have it down perfectly, and I don't have all the answers. But by the grace of God we'll continue to grow together toward him and each other.

I think it is wonderful that God can use all of us, regardless of our personality type or gifting. God loves the motivated go-getters, the thoughtful job-completers, the sensitive problem-solvers. I am thankful for who God made me to be, and how he continues to mold me. I am excited to see where he is leading me in my relationship with my husband and children, and in areas of ministry. Life is a challenge, but also a joyful experience. We need to look expectantly at each day as a day that we are being used by God. I am eternally grateful for all God has done for me and his great love for us all.

Pat's Responses to Chapter Questions

.....

Chapter 1

1. Many people would argue that the Internet is evil. What do you believe about it and other technologies that have been used in questionable manners?

I believe that the Internet, like most everything in this world, can be used for good and, sadly, for evil as well. I'm personally excited about the enormous ministry potentials for the Net. For instance, we can use it to give the finest training and teaching to new church leaders everywhere on the globe. Maybe this tool will play a vital role in reaching all people groups for Christ.

2. Chester Carlson, the founder of Xerox, attributed his sustenance during difficult times to the *Bhagavad Gita*, a Hindu spiritual text. Do you think that being spiritual is important, whether you are a Christian, Hindu, or Muslim?

There's great value in each of the major religions. While I've not studied each of them in depth, I find there is a great deal of commonality in the morality and ethics they each teach. I expect serious students and participants in any of them will lead more fulfilled lives and have powerful personal and professional careers as a result. As I've met and become acquainted or even have gained close friends with people from many religions, I can offer firsthand evidence that this is the case.

At the same time, I make no apologies for my personal faith in Christ

Jesus and him alone. I believe Christianity to be unique. I believe Christ is the singular way to heaven (Acts 4:12), and it is Christ's death on the cross by which every human being is offered a path to heaven. We are all sinners (Rom. 3:23). We all deserved eternal death (Rom. 6:23). We are uniquely saved by grace (Rom. 3:24) through Christ's blood (Eph. 2:13, 1 Peter 1:18–19). If we have faith in him (Rom. 10:13) and repent of our sins and are baptized into him (Acts 2:38), we will receive his Holy Spirit (Acts 2:38) and eternal life (Rom. 6:23).

While I respect that many who read this may be of Hindu or Muslim or other faiths, I can only pray that you would consider thoughtfully the unique claims of Christ as Savior and Lord. You can't consider him a great prophet or teacher and then ignore what he said. He claimed to be the Son of God.

3. In your time with God, do you ask him for help with your work or profession? Does God provide ideas, witty inventions, or specific help in the workplace? Do you have some ways to know how to proceed, such as what direction to take in your work?

Yes, we should be in constant communication with God in all areas of our lives (Phil. 4:6). I recall an instance when I asked my Bible-study group for prayers for a difficult exam I was facing. A man of the church chided me about my request. He felt it was inappropriate to bring such trivial matters before God, particularly if I had properly studied for the exam. I disagreed with him at the time and strongly disagree today. We should bring all the requests and concerns of our daily lives before God. I've taken every major chip, project, organization, business, or technology I've worked on for over twenty years at Intel before the throne of God. I suggest you do the same with your work as well.

4. Maybe you feel like you are working as hard as you can just to keep pace; you aren't a type-A overachiever and regularly need more sleep than Pat does. How do you achieve balance in life even though you consider yourself a more "normal" person?

All biblical principles apply to all people regardless of their intelligence level, race, sex, skill, or role they are in. "Brilliant" people don't have fewer demands on them. In fact, the opposite is often true—the more gifted you are, the more opportunities you are provided to use those gifts. I'd point to Matthew 25 as a teaching of Jesus that confirms this point, or again in Luke 12:48: "From everyone who has been given much, much will be demanded; and from the one who has been entrusted with much, much more will be asked."

As a gifted person, you will have increased demands placed upon you to produce fruit. Also, the picture of the parable of the master and talents communicates that as you succeed with what talents you have, God will provide you with greater opportunities.

Each of us should constantly be looking for ways and roles where God can use our unique gifts. Balancing our time becomes more of a challenge the more we do that. Thus, the principles and guidelines in this book apply to all *people who are being challenged with balance in the workplace.*

5. How do you know if you are in the right profession? Could a struggle with balance occur because you are doing the wrong thing?

Knowing the will of God for your life is a difficult challenge for anyone. I'd point to Romans 12:2:

> *Do not conform any longer to the pattern of this world, but be*

transformed by the renewing of your mind. Then you will be able to test
and approve what God's will is—his good, pleasing and perfect will.

Clearly and consistently pursuing Christ will open up an
understanding of your gifts and how he can use you. At some point, a
job or career change may be appropriate. Often, just learning to make
him Lord and working for him as we discussed in chapter 5 will make
your current role far more fulfilling and satisfying. Soon after I became a
Christian, I felt compelled to leave technology and go into the ministry.
I struggled with this for many months. I finally "laid a fleece before
God" as Gideon had done in Judges 6 when he was seeking the Lord's
direction. My fleece has remained dry to this day, and I consider this a
clear answer from God that my ministry wasn't in leaving the workplace
and career I was in. Since then I've grown to see how God can use my
current profession and role in mighty ways for his kingdom. As such, I'm
confident I'm exactly where God wants me to be—at least for now.

Chapter 2

1. Why do you really need to prepare a personal mission statement
with specific values and goals?

If you haven't yet created one, please do. If you've taken the time to get
this far into the book, it is a must-do. As we've tried to develop through
chapter 2, a mission statement is a starting point to setting a long-term
direction for your life. What do you want to do with what you have left
of your gift of time from God? What legacy will you leave on earth? It's
like a compass for the decisions we need to make every day.

2. What kinds of time-management tools do you use?

You can find a variety of time-management tools and systems. Some are computer based, and some attempt to integrate priorities and goals as well as time management. Over the years, I've used many with varying success. At different points in my professional career, different tools have been more or less appropriate.

Generally, my simple conclusion is that it doesn't matter which tool you use or how you use them. The important point is having a personal mission statement, periodically assessing your time, and putting in place some mechanisms to keep you living consistently with your goals. After you have your mission statement developed and in place, it is pretty easy to integrate the priorities that you have into any of the time-management tools available to you today.

3. How can you set goals or mission statements when the world around us changes so fast?

Of course, your personal mission statement will change over time, and you should periodically update and refine it. However, as you try to write your mission statement, make the goals longer term and not too specific to an individual assignment or role. After completing mine about seven years ago, I've needed to make only minor modifications since.

4. How should you go about developing a will and detailed financial plan for your family?

People often do these as they consider their lives and plans more seriously. It isn't morbid to consider what happens when you die; it's prudent to plan for your family. Depending on the complexity of your estate and finances, you might be able to do these on your own with books or PC software that are now readily available. If your situation is more complicated, you may need to hire professionals such as a lawyer or financial planner. You will probably also want to update these every five to ten years to reflect your changing circumstances. Linda and I recently updated our wills that we had developed about seven years ago.

5. If you haven't started writing your personal mission statement, do a first draft right now. Use the three-section example given in this chapter as a model. Share the results with your spouse, mentor, or close friend.

As we've discussed in this chapter, this is hard work, and you should expect to spend some quality time contemplating your long-term goals for life. Finally, my prayers are with you as you get started on this plan for life!

Chapter 3

1. How can you make and keep God your number one priority in life?

It is intensely difficult to put and then keep God on the throne of our lives in the face of so many activities, demands, and priorities. Having daily devotions, staying active in the local church, and letting mentors keep you accountable are some steps in the right direction.

2. Do you find your religious regimen ever getting to the point where it is little more than a daily routine? How can you put more of yourself into your personal devotions and prayer?

Yes, daily devotions can become routine. There are great resource materials to help us, however. The Necessity of Prayer *by E. M. Bounds is maybe the greatest reference on the subject. Here are other ideas I've found useful:*

Position is important. I cannot pray sitting for very long; I daydream or sleep. I can pray standing or on my knees.

I am much more effective praying aloud than silently. Silently, my mind tends to wander. Aloud, it seems more personal and focused. I often pray when I'm driving, and if I do so out loud it can be an especially effective time of communication with God.

I follow the simple ACTS outline: Adoration or Acknowledge God (that is, praise him, thank him), Confess my sins (be specific and thorough), Thanksgiving (Christ, family, his provision, etc.), and finally Supplication (your list of requests, needs, and areas for his intervention).

I find it useful to hum or sing praise songs as I pray, particularly when I'm in the "Acknowledge or Adoration" portion. Singing tends to take me into his presence and keep me there. Pray for a while, sing a song, pray some more, sing again, pray again. Using Scripture directly in your prayers is powerful as well.

Pray frequently. What I've outlined above is my once-a-day major time in devotions. However, often I find the greatest prayers to be those quick, spur-of-the-moment prayers. Pray when you are walking into a meeting, when you are driving to work, when you see a need, and when you don't know what to say in a particular situation (Phil. 4:6).

3. Is it wise for someone who travels heavily or puts in late nights at work to commit to leading a weekly Bible study? How can you fit your home Bible study into an already taxing schedule?

Prioritizing church activities is part of your commitment to God. Your work schedule may require those activities to occur on weekends. However, depending on your job requirements, having a home study may or may not be a good decision. Maybe leading a class on Sundays or a study on weekends or at lunchtime at the workplace would be more suitable.

In my case, I make an effort to be home on Wednesday evenings. However, due to business travel and other activities, I can't always make it. I have a friend, Ed, who worked with me on the study and was ready to fill in for me whenever required.

4. How can you make your finances reflect God as the highest priority in your life?

Throughout the Old and New Testaments, we see a call to a life of giving to the Lord's work. As is the case with most laws and requirements of the Old Testament, they are replaced with loftier ideals and principles in the New Testament. The Bible has an awful lot to say about finances, which can't be ignored. Moving toward a life of sacrifice, blessing, inheritance, and agreement is a lifelong journey of financial stewardship that can be challenging but also extraordinarily rewarding both for now and for eternity.

5. How do you deal with work assigned to you on a Sunday?

Two thoughts:

Maybe some will disagree with me here, but I believe we are entirely under the new covenant. Thus, I don't believe we have a Sabbath law that we are required to obey. Throughout the New Testament we see Jesus at odds with the Pharisees over this exact point. However, the New Testament also calls for the consistent coming together in worship of believers. Thus, I wouldn't be too concerned about working on Sundays as long as you are in a worship service weekly. For example, some churches offer a Saturday-evening service for this exact reason. However, this "freedom" may not make you particularly comfortable and perhaps you just need to be in worship on Sundays. In that case, obey your conscience and find a position that allows this to be the case.

The Sabbath concept—the call to a time of rest and focus on God—remains valid and important. Preserving and enjoying such time is part of a healthy balance in one's life.

If you aren't able to consistently maintain balance and be in worship on a weekly basis, you should probably consider a different position where this can be the case.

Chapter 4

1. How can you prioritize your spouse above your children and profession?

Both you and your spouse need to discuss this question thoughtfully. Explore where you might be letting the many demands of the kids or your job crowd your spouse out of his or her proper place in your life. What specific actions can you take to clearly communicate that your spouse, next to your relationship with God, is the most important relationship you have on this earth? There are some excellent resources available in your local Christian bookstore that deal specifically with this topic.

2. Are regular dates with your spouse really necessary? Why?

This is a critical step in establishing your priorities. Through dating, taking weekends away together, and focused communication on a regular basis, you can build an ongoing, ever-deepening relationship with your spouse. When your children leave the home, you and your spouse will remain. Will you still know each other? Will you be more deeply in love with each other the day the last child leaves the nest than the day the two of you wed?

3. How can you make family time a priority in your regular weekly activities?

Some of the tools we've suggested, like one-on-one times during the week with each kid or a weekend checklist, will help. Find ways such as family vacations to create those memories that you and each member of your family will cherish for years to come. Invest the time in "family nights," in which everyone is required not to have any extra activities. The family has dinner together and spends the evening playing games and enjoying other activities together.

4. How does your spouse manage alone with the kids when you're away?

Linda is a wonderful mother and tremendous support. Obviously she is blessed by God in her role as well. I also need to encourage her regularly and express my appreciation and gratitude. This is where things such as dating, gifts, cards, letters, and numerous other expressions of both love and gratitude are vital. I pray for her daily too.

5. How would you handle a spouse who is intensely busy, gone a lot, not involved in a church or the family, and not responsive to your suggestions to alter his or her priorities?

As with any situation, begin by taking the situation before God. Your job as a wife or husband is to be entirely supportive in all situations and for whatever length of time is required (Eph. 5:22–24; Col. 3:19; 1 Peter 3:1–6). The husband's job is almost exactly parallel to that of the wife in each of these passages (Eph. 5:25–28; Col. 3:20–22; 1 Peter 3:7). You can gently encourage your spouse to consider Scripture passages such as these; you might also ask him or her to read this book. If your mate is not a Christian, of course, your primary goal is to gently bring him or her to see Christ through both your lifestyle and your verbal witness (1 Peter 3:1).

6. If your spouse is an extreme workaholic or simply refuses to adjust priorities, what can you do to improve the situation?

Difficult situations like this seldom have easy answers.

Of course, pray for your spouse to be open to change. With humility and an appealing spirit, continue to suggest change. While I have made adjustments over the years to my life and work balance, Linda's direct promptings—not random complaints or expressions of frustration—often have been the impetus for me to make changes. Since I'm still far from perfect, I am certain she will continue to encourage me to grow and improve my juggling skills.

You could also seek to discuss the situation with others whom your spouse respects and might listen to. Consider the possibility of counseling help as well.

As suggested by the answer to question 5, you always need to remain supportive of your spouse, even in situations like this. This is easy to say but most difficult to do when your spouse is making obvious and painful mistakes, hurting your relationship and the family. However, that is exactly what the Scriptures call you to do.

Finally, while you can't change your spouse, you can change yourself. Make sure you are correctly prioritizing your life and your relationship with your spouse even if he or she isn't yet doing so.

Chapter 5

1. How do you handle work commitments that come into conflict with family commitments?

While I gave a few examples in the text, I have often put my family commitments above work demands. I am certain these conflicts will continue to arise, and I'm certain I will put family first many times. I would caution you not to be dogmatic about this in either direction. Sometimes a high-priority work assignment will arise when you had a family commitment that was not particularly critical. Do your work assignment, and do it well. Other times a modest work assignment will conflict with a family commitment; please honor the family commitment. Of course, the difficult situations are when there's a high-priority work assignment and an important family commitment. In these circumstances, keep the family commitment and be prepared for the potential consequences at work. Hopefully, by being a great employee, you will have established a strong balance in your invisible value account and can weather such situations with ease.

2. How can you manage when projects become intense and short target dates are set—when it becomes difficult to please family and friends while still being an effective employee?

The challenge of short target dates sometimes causes us to make choices that leave family time short. In the day and age of the Internet and mobile communications, demands come seven days a week, twenty-four hours a day. Many of our industries are global, making 24/7 a fact, not a phrase. Thus, these periods are to be expected and are often required. Make these trade-offs and continue being a great employee. However, you must follow those intense work times with balancing times spent with family and friends.

Also, some jobs will turn into one intense period followed by another and another and so on. If these periods of intensity can never be balanced with family and God, you need to look at making more significant adjustments to your work and agenda, possibly even considering a new position in the company.

3. In an environment where corruption is a way to achieve goals, how can one maintain integrity?

There is no room for corruption in the Christian life. As believers, we are constantly challenged by the Bible to live holy lives (2 Peter 3:11). However, there is a fine line between doing your job as directed, aware that there may be corruption about you, and participating directly in corruption. It isn't your job or role to seek out corruption or questionable ethics. However, when you are confronted with ethic violations or corruption, you are obligated as a Christian to take appropriate steps to address it. Being a beacon of light in the midst of a corrupt world is what we are called to do as Christians (Matt. 5:13–16). This is where being a great employee, working hard, and yet living a moral and godly life can be the most powerful witness a Christian businessperson can have.

4. Would you continue to work hard even if you came across unethical behavior in your company?

Absolutely. Remember that you work for God first and foremost (Col. 3:23). To make this point even more forcefully, look to 1 Peter 2:17, where Peter urges Christians to "honor the king." In Peter's day, the kings were none other than the evil Roman Caesars, who were persecuting the Christians and outlawing Christianity. Despite this extreme corruption, Peter urges respect and honor to the king who is in power only due to God's sovereign command. In fact, depending on the date of Peter's writing, the king at the time could have been Nero, who burned Christians at the stake to light his courts at night.

Thus, the principle is powerful: Work hard, as working for the Lord, despite the circumstances around you.

5. A bad economy puts a lot of pressure in our work lives. Where should one draw the line in terms of commitments and responsibilities?

Times of pressure are when priorities and balance are more important than ever. We learn far more in difficult times or times of failure than we do in times of ease or success.

6. How do you see the trade-off between working to fill the pockets of another individual and earning a living for yourself?

Work in its entirety is from God. We see this since the fall of man, when God ordained man to work to sustain life (Gen. 3:19). Not only was it instituted by God at this early time, but we see it consistently required through the Old Testament and the New as well (2 Thess. 3:10). Most of the great men and women of the Bible had professions before or in addition to their roles in ministry. Some worked independently (e.g., as shepherds or fishermen), others had bosses (e.g., tax collectors), and some were slaves (e.g., Philemon). But in all cases, the principles of work ethics seem to be asserted and applied (Col. 3:23).

Of course, some jobs seem inappropriate for Christians (bars, pornography, gambling). Thus, except for directly immoral positions, the key issue is not what kind of work you do or what kind of employer you have, but whether you're living a godly and holy life.

7. How often do you review your time chart?

Typically I update it monthly and have kept a history of over ten years of results, which is helpful to see trends. Often, I have consistently difficult or busy periods of the year. Looking at a year helps me know these are coming up and helps me to work especially hard at being home either before or after those particularly busy periods.

Chapter 6

1. How might you go about finding a mentor?

Carefully consider what areas you want to improve or grow in. Then look for people you trust and respect who are strong in those areas. Finally, make your desire known and ask for a commitment of adequate time. Also, seek out those for whom you might be a mentor. Develop relationships where you can help others mature in their professional and spiritual lives.

2. What should you do in your mentoring time? How often should you meet?

In a busy professional career, it's hard to give a simple prescription for how often to meet. Trying to meet once a week is a great goal, and I probably average once every two weeks currently. If you meet less than once per month, the relationship is probably becoming ineffective. During your time, you might work through a specific Bible study together that is relevant to the areas in which you want to develop. Currently I've been using Knowing God. *You might just meet to talk about things going on in your life. At a minimum keep track of prayer requests and specific topics in some form of journal between your meetings.*

3. What do you think about having more than one mentor? How many mentors should one have?

If you have a Paul, a Barnabas, and a Timothy in both your professional life and in your spiritual life, you would have six. If you had several ad hoc relationships as well, you might have a few more. Generally, I've never been able to maintain that many at one time and would advise against trying to do so. I try to have one mentor/Paul, one I'm mentoring/Timothy, and one accountability partner/Barnabas.

Of course for some, just having one mentor is a big step forward. If you've never had any before, I'd strongly encourage you to start with just one mentor or peer as a starting point. After you've matured and developed in this way, you might be ready for a second.

4. How can you mentor team members at work or employees that report to you?

Mentoring is primarily a decision of the mentee and not the mentor. And while you can encourage those in your work family to seek and take such guidance, you cannot force it or require it. When I mentor people in my group, I take care not to show or even give the appearance of favoritism. I try to function as a coach to the individual, just as I would for most anyone on the team, and I encourage the person to find other mentors as well. Intel's open-door policy helps too; if any staff felt slighted, he or she could air a complaint to anyone above me in the chain of command.

5. Can you think of three people who would make good "Paul," "Timothy," and "Barnabas" roles in your life? Write down their names and commit to approach them about a mentoring relationship as the first step to weave your life together with theirs.

Spend some quality time thinking and praying about the individuals you put on your list. You are asking them to help you, and further, you want to make sure you make good and godly choices for such important roles in your life.

Chapter 7

1. How can you take opportunities to share God's Word at work? How would you do so? Are there any specific examples where you've been able to do so?

Your first witness in the workplace is being a great employee. If you don't do that, you will diminish any level of witness you might have.

Your second witness is your lifestyle and ethics. Do you conduct your life with the highest of morals and ethics, or do you casually participate in corrupt or questionable behavior? Do you participate in crude discussions or joking? Do people see you having your personal devotions during your breaks and lunch hours?

Third, you will get opportunities to express concern for others in a godly and genuine way. If a coworker is ill or has lost a family member, an "I'll be thinking of and praying for you," a gift of flowers, or a genuine "I'll come over and help you during your time of need" will speak volumes.

Finally, you may be afforded the occasional opportunity to witness verbally to others. This needs to be done with great prudence, lest you ever gain the reputation of using work time to proselytize others. This is also why I put such emphasis on being a "great employee" and putting your professional character above reproach. You must be even more cautious not to allow your position as a supervisor to place pressure on a subordinate in this regard. You should never witness during work time, only during breaks or off time.

A specific example might be a recent instance where a coworker's girlfriend fell unexpectedly ill and quickly died. Given the three points above, I had a great opportunity to talk with him about faith in Christ in a casual yet profound way.

2. Under what circumstances would it be inappropriate to witness at your job?

As suggested in the answer to the last question, you can always witness through your work and character. Expressing concern should be done as the occasions allow and as often as God brings them your way. I would suggest caution in being too bold with witnessing at your job until you've developed a balance in your value account. Also, be careful of any policies your company might have in this regard. As already covered, never let your desire to witness become a distraction to being a great employee. Finally, beware of witnessing during your normal work hours. It's a matter of Christian integrity and being a living witness that those hours be focused on your work. Christians need to be above reproach in every regard.

3. What makes you uncomfortable in sharing your faith? What steps can you think of to help address those areas? Practice sharing your faith with your mentor or a Christian friend. Get to the point where you are comfortable with some simple discussion points about your faith.

One of the best ways to get comfortable sharing your faith is simply practicing doing so. Sharing your faith doesn't need to be hard, it's simply telling people about your relationship with Jesus. What were the circumstances that brought you to this point? What does Christ mean to you today? How has he changed your life?

While it is great to invite people to Christian functions, wonderful to invite them to join you at church, and always great to be a good friend, none of those are sharing your faith. Practice with a friend and get comfortable with the simple idea of sharing Christ with another.

4. If one is not a Christian, can he or she still go about bringing balance to life?

I do believe that the only true balance one can find in life is through Christ. Nevertheless, most of the tools in these chapters can still be applied (as is the case with many Christian truths). Chapters 3 and 7 are pretty specific to Christians and those of faith. Even in those cases, though, most of the practical advice in the other chapters will still be useful. But consider this premise: If it is useful and true, consider the source.

5. What are some practical situations that are going on in your life right now where you feel you should be a Christian witness but haven't had the courage to do so?

Maybe it is someone with a profane tendency, like the situation I described with Andy Grove. Maybe it's a colleague you've worked with for many years and you've never simply come out and told them they need to know Christ. Where is the Holy Spirit prompting you right now to stop delaying and to finally take action? Write your answers down and tell them to your spouse, mentor, or such, and ask him or her to hold you accountable.

Chapter 8

1. Do you have ethics situations in the workplace that you feel like you need to address?

As discussed in this chapter, be a role model, be aware of your business's corporate and legal requirements, and don't be the self-appointed ethics investigator. However, if in the course of doing your job you see situations that seem wrong, document them factually and bring them to the appropriate individual's awareness.

2. Do you consider yourself a "full-time minister" in the workplace? Why or why not?

While this is a simple idea, some might struggle with the concept of your workplace as your full-time mission field. As I described in chapter 5, you need to be a great employee. You aren't called to spend your hours at the water cooler talking about Christ. You are there to honor Jesus Christ by being a great employee. However, while you are doing that, you have a platform—a set of relationships that God wants you to use for eternal purposes.

3. What are some simple rules for circumstances where you would or wouldn't share your faith in the workplace?

As I suggest in this chapter, I think two are particularly useful: Be yourself, and if the other person goes to the personal level, so can you. Are there others that you've found useful in your life?

4. What are some practical steps for how you would be able to be a Christian witness in the workplace?

Your attitude, more than anything else, will influence your effectiveness. If you approach others with humility, respect, and heartfelt concern, coworkers will generally give great deference to the message you have to offer.

Also, being a clear witness is best done where a relationship already exists. *First, develop that relationship, and then build and expand to other areas of your life, including your faith.*

Being a witness is often done in trivial ways of what you say or how you react to a situation. Reacting in a godly way to a difficult circumstance might be the most powerful witness you'll ever have. For instance, I make it a point to carry a joyous demeanor even in difficult times. As people ask what I'm happy about, I can often share more of my life and faith.

5. In what areas do you see your integrity being challenged? What are some practical steps to avoid those challenges? What are some Scriptures that might address those challenges?

For many years, my performance reviews at Intel said I needed to work on my peer relationships. I was seen as using others to get ahead. I didn't share the limelight nor did I invest heavily in interpersonal relationships. My reaction to these comments was modest at best and often out of those struggles emanated all sorts of political issues, which certainly tested my integrity. Similarly, in another challenge, as a male with two eyes, I wasn't honoring Linda fully, which easily opened the door for lustful thoughts. With ruthless honesty, what are your challenges? Are you willing to adjust your character, your lifestyle, and be transparent to others?

6. What are some practical suggestions for being a witness through your job?

On one flight I had a ton of work to do. As soon as the plane reached 10,000 feet, I went to work. The guy next to me, though, wanted to chat. Finally, after multiple attempts to ignore him, I just gave up and thought, Okay, God, I'll talk to him about you. *If he wasn't going to let me work, he* was *going to hear the gospel. Too often, we are just so busy we don't heed the God-given appointments that he has arranged for us. I am terribly guilty of this one.*

Also, take every opportunity that the little things afford. When someone is sick, ask, "Can I pray for you?" If someone has struggled with a divorce, come alongside them, offer to pray for them and their children, and inquire of any practical need you can help with. One coworker came to Christ in the midst of his divorce. He was delighted to tell me one day, "Hey, Pat, I got wet." At first I wasn't sure what he was talking about, and then I realized he was baptized that prior week! He and his two daughters remain on my regular prayer list today.

7. Are you an integrated person when you show up for work? The same person that you are in your home and place of worship? If not, what steps can you take to start bringing yourself into harmony?

Think for a moment on the things you say and do at work. Would you mind if your family was there watching you? Your minister? Your Savior? If there are any examples that come to mind, jot them down and think about some practical steps that you might take to change those behaviors. Do you see your job as a role you have as ordained by God? Can you see how God is working through you today for his ultimate kingdom and glory? What can you do to increase your passion and enthusiasm for your job? Do you need to consider a different role where you can use the talents God has given you?

Notes

· · · · ·

1. Bob Buford, *Half Time* (Grand Rapids, MI: Zondervan, 1994).

2. John Crawford and Patrick Gelsinger, *Programming the 80386* (Alameda, CA: Sybex, 1987).

3. Encyclopedia Britannica, *1999 Britannica Book of the Year.*

4. Randy Alcorn, *The Treasure Principle* (Sisters, OR: Lifechange Books, 2001).

5. David McLaughlin, *The Role of the Man in the Family* (Neenah, WI: David McLaughlin video series).

6. Two sources recommended:

Seven Promises of a Promise Keeper (Colorado Springs: Focus on the Family, 1994), 47–67.

Howard Hendricks and William Hendricks, *As Iron Sharpens Iron* (Chicago: Moody, 1995).

7. "Enron," Wikipedia, http://en.wikipedia.org/wiki/Enron (accessed June 18, 2008).

73717750R00154

Made in the
USA
Middletown, DE